1980s Project Studies/Council on Foreign Relations

STUDIES AVAILABLE

DIVERSITY AND DEVELOPMENT IN SOUTHEAST ASIA:
The Coming Decade
Studies by Guy J. Pauker, Frank H. Golay, and Cynthia H. Enloe

NUCLEAR WEAPONS AND WORLD POLITICS:
Alternatives for the Future
Studies by David C. Gompert, Michael Mandelbaum, Richard L. Garwin, and John H. Barton

CHINA'S FUTURE:
Foreign Policy and Economic Development in the Post-Mao Era
Studies by Allen S. Whiting and by Robert F. Dernberger

ALTERNATIVES TO MONETARY DISORDER
Studies by Fred Hirsch and Michael W. Doyle and by Edward L. Morse

NUCLEAR PROLIFERATION:
Motivations, Capabilities, and Strategies for Control
Studies by Ted Greenwood and by Harold A. Feiveson and Theodore B. Taylor

INTERNATIONAL DISASTER RELIEF:
Toward a Responsive System
Stephen Green

STUDIES FORTHCOMING

Some 20 additional volumes of the 1980s Project work will be appearing in the course of the next year or two. Most will contain independent but related studies concerning issues of potentially great importance in the next decade and beyond, such as resource management, terrorism, relations between the developing and developed societies, and the world market in conventional arms, among many others. Additionally, a number of volumes will be devoted to particular regions of the world, concentrating especially on political and economic development trends outside the industrialized West.

Diversity and Development in Southeast Asia

Diversity and Development in Southeast Asia

THE COMING DECADE

GUY J. PAUKER

FRANK H. GOLAY

CYNTHIA H. ENLOE

Introduction by Catherine Gwin

1980s Project/Council on Foreign Relations

McGRAW-HILL BOOK COMPANY

New York   St. Louis   San Francisco
Auckland   Bogotá   Düsseldorf   Johannesburg   London   Madrid
Mexico   Montreal   New Delhi   Panama   Paris   São Paulo
Singapore   Sydney   Tokyo   Toronto

The Council on Foreign Relations, Inc., is a nonprofit and nonpartisan organization devoted to promoting improved understanding of international affairs through the free exchange of ideas. Its membership of about 1,700 persons throughout the United States is made up of individuals with special interest and experience in international affairs. The Council has no affiliation with and receives no funding from the United States government.

The Council publishes the quarterly journal *Foreign Affairs* and, from time to time, books and monographs that in the judgment of the Council's Committee on Studies are responsible treatments of significant international topics worthy of presentation to the public. The 1980s Project is a research effort of the Council; as such, 1980s Project Studies have been similarly reviewed through procedures of the Committee on Studies. As in the case of all Council publications, statements of fact and expressions of opinion contained in 1980s Project Studies are the sole responsibility of their authors.

The editor of this book was Susan Sorrell for the Council on Foreign Relations. Thomas Quinn and Michael Hennelly were the editors for McGraw-Hill Book Company. Christopher Simon was the designer. Teresa Leaden supervised the production. This book was set in Times Roman by Creative Book Services, Inc.

Printed and bound by R. R. Donnelley & Sons.

Library of Congress Cataloging in Publication Data
Pauker, Guy J
Diversity and development in Southeast Asia.

(1980's project/Council on Foreign Relations)
Bibliography: p.
Includes index.
1. Regionalism—Asia, Southeastern. 2. Asia, South-
eastern—Economic integration. 3. Asia, Southeastern—
Economic policy. I. Golay, Frank H., joint author.
II. Enloe, Cynthia H., joint author.
III. Title. IV. Series: Council on Foreign Relations.
1980's Project/Council on Foreign Relations.
HT395.A85P38   330.9'59   77-23441
ISBN 0-07-048917-3
ISBN 0-07-048918-1 pbk.

1 2 3 4 5 6 7 8 9 R R D R R D 7 0 9 8 7

Contents

Foreword: The 1980s Project

These explorations of the likely paths of economic and political development of the nations of Southeast Asia and of the roles that Southeast Asian states might play in world politics are part of a stream of studies to be produced in the course of the 1980s Project of the Council on Foreign Relations. Each Project study analyzes an issue or set of issues that is likely to be of international concern during the next 10 to 20 years.

The ambitious purpose of the 1980s Project is to examine important political and economic problems not only individually but in relationship to one another. Some studies or books produced by the Project will primarily emphasize the interrelationship of issues. In the case of other, more specifically focused studies, a considerable effort has been made to write, review, and criticize them in the context of more general Project work. Each Project study is thus capable of standing on its own; at the same time it has been shaped by a broader perspective.

The 1980s Project had its origins in the widely held recognition that many of the assumptions, policies, and institutions that have characterized international relations during the past 30 years are inadequate to the demands of today and the foreseeable demands of the period between now and 1990 or so. Over the course of the next decade, substantial adaptation of institutions and behavior will be needed to respond to the changed circumstances of the 1980s and beyond. The Project seeks to identify those future conditions and the kinds of adaptation they might require. It is not the Project's purpose to arrive at a single or exclusive set of goals. Nor does it focus upon the foreign policy or national interests of the United States alone. Instead, it seeks to identify goals that are compatible with the perceived interests of most states, despite differences in ideology and in level of economic development.

The published products of the Project are aimed at a broad readership, including policy makers and potential policy makers and those who would influence the policy-making process, but are confined to no single nation or region. The authors of Project studies were therefore asked to remain mindful of interests broader than those of any one society and to take fully into account the likely realities of domestic politics in the principal societies involved. All those who have worked in the Project, however, have tried not to be captives of the status quo; they have sought to question the inevitability of existing patterns of thought and behavior that restrain desirable change and to look for ways in which those patterns might in time be altered or their consequences mitigated.

The 1980s Project is at once a series of separate attacks upon a number of urgent and potentially urgent international problems and also a collective effort, involving a substantial number of persons in the United States and abroad, to bring those separate approaches to bear upon one another and to suggest the kinds of choices that might be made among them. The Project involves more than 300 participants. A small central staff and a steering Coordinating Group have worked to define the questions and to assess the compatibility of policy prescriptions. Nearly 100 authors, from more than a dozen countries, have been at work on separate studies. Ten working groups of specialists and generalists have been convened to subject the Project's studies to critical scrutiny and to help in the process of identifying interrelationships among them.

The 1980s Project is the largest single research and studies effort the Council on Foreign Relations has undertaken in its 55-year history, comparable in conception only to a major study of the postwar world, the War and Peace Studies, undertaken by the Council during the Second World War. At that time, the impetus to the effort was the discontinuity caused by worldwide conflict and visible and inescapable need to rethink, replace, and supplement many of the features of the international system that had prevailed before the war. The discontinuities in today's world are less obvious and, even when occasionally quite visible—as in the abandonment of gold convertibility and fixed monetary parities—only briefly command the spotlight of public attention. That new institutions and patterns of behavior are needed in many areas is widely acknowledged, but the sense of need is less urgent—existing institutions have not for the most part dramatically failed and collapsed. The tendency, therefore, is to make do with outmoded arrangements and to improvise rather than to undertake a basic analysis of the problems that lie before us and of the demands that those problems will place upon all nations.

The 1980s Project is based upon the belief that serious effort and integrated forethought can contribute—indeed, are indispensable—to progress in the next decade toward a more humane, peaceful, productive, and just world. And it rests upon the hope that participants in its deliberations and readers of Project publications—whether or not they agree with an author's point of view—may be helped to think more informedly about the opportunities and the dangers that lie ahead and the consequences of various possible courses of future action.

The 1980s Project has been made possible by generous grants from the Ford Foundation, the Lilly Endowment, the Andrew W. Mellon Foundation, the Rockefeller Foundation, and the German Marshall Fund of the United States. Neither the Council on Foreign Relations nor any of the foundations is responsible for statements of fact and expressions of opinion contained in publications of the 1980s Project; they are the sole responsibility of the individual authors under whose names they appear. But the Council on Foreign Relations and the staff of the 1980s Project take great pleasure in placing those publications before a wide readership both in the United States and abroad.

Edward L. Morse and Richard H. Ullman

1980s PROJECT WORKING GROUP

During 1975 and 1976, ten Working Groups met to explore major international issues and to subject initial drafts of 1980s Project studies to critical review. Those who chaired Project Working Groups were:

Cyrus R. Vance, Working Group on Nuclear Weapons and Other Weapons of Mass Destruction

Leslie H. Gelb, Working Group on Armed Conflict

Roger Fisher, Working Group on Transnational Violence and Subversion

Rev. Theodore M. Hesburgh, Working Group on Human Rights

Joseph S. Nye, Jr., Working Group on the Political Economy of North-South Relations

Harold Van B. Cleveland, Working Group on Macroeconomic Policies and International Monetary Relations

Lawrence C. McQuade, Working Group on Principles of International Trade

William Diebold, Jr., Working Group on Multinational Enterprises

Eugene B. Skolnikoff, Working Group on the Environment, the Global Commons, and Economic Growth

Miriam Camps, Working Group on Industrial Policy

1980s PROJECT STAFF

Persons who have held senior professional positions on the staff for all or part of its duration are:

Miriam Camps	*Catherine Gwin*
William Diebold Jr.	*Roger D. Hansen*
Tom J. Farer	*Edward L. Morse*
David C. Gompert	*Richard H. Ullman*

Richard H. Ullman was Director of the 1980s Project from its inception in 1974 until July 1977 when he became Chairman of the Project Coordinating Group. At that time, Edward L. Morse became Executive Director of the Project.

PROJECT COORDINATING GROUP

The Coordinating Group of the 1980s Project has had a central advisory role in the work of the Project. Its members as of December 31, 1976, were:

W. Michael Blumenthal
Richard N. Cooper
Carlos F. Diaz-Alejandro
Richard A. Falk
Tom J. Farer
Edward K. Hamilton
Stanley Hoffmann
Samuel P. Huntington
Gordon J. MacDonald
Bruce K. MacLaury

Bayless Manning
Theodore R. Marmor
Ali Mazrui
Joseph S. Nye, Jr.
Michael O'Neill
Marshall D. Shulman
Stephen Stamas
Fritz Stern
Allen S. Whiting

COMMITTEE ON STUDIES

The Committee on Studies of the Board of Directors of the Council on Foreign Relations is the governing body of the 1980s Project. The Committee's members as of December 31, 1976, were:

W. Michael Blumenthal
Zbigniew Brzezinski
Robert A. Charpie
Richard N. Cooper

Walter J. Levy
Joseph S. Nye, Jr.
Robert V. Roosa
Carroll L. Wilson

James A. Perkins (Chairman)

Diversity and Development in Southeast Asia

Southeast Asia in the 1980s

Catherine Gwin

During the past few years the claims of poor nations against rich nations have increasingly dominated world politics. In their efforts to press for a restructuring of international economic relations and institutions, developing states have drawn attention to the disparity of wealth and power among nations, the failure of economic development to reach the very poor, and the complex ways in which interdependence poses risks for weak nations. These issues are certain to remain critical ones in world politics during the 1980s. What is less certain, however, is the extent to which the capacities, goals, and priorities of developed and developing nations may diverge during that period and, thus, whether the international system will be made more or less conducive to development and peace.

This volume is one of five in the 1980s Project dealing with political, economic, and sociocultural factors underlying present and projected trends within developing countries.[1] One principal task of the essays in these volumes, which are grouped according to geographic region, is to examine the similarities and differences characterizing developing countries, which collectively have come to be called the "South." The purpose of this effort is to shed light on two closely related features of the South: the sources and strengths of the commitment of individual states to join with

[1] Forthcoming volumes will focus on the Middle East and North Africa, Latin America, South Asia, and Africa.

others to press for political and economic change and the ways in which Southern perceptions of development problems will affect the kinds of claims that developing states will make in the decade ahead. By describing and analyzing these features, this series of regional studies complements evaluations of desirable changes in North-South relations contained in other volumes of the Project.[2]

In addition, the essays in each volume assess the prospects for conflict or accommodation among communal groups in each region and evaluate the potential for increased regional cooperation as a means of accelerating national development, enhancing national security, and fostering regional stability. Thus, the volumes address several concrete and related questions stemming from the ways in which political and economic developments on three levels—national, regional, and international—affect and are affected by developments on each of the other levels.

In organizing these studies of states of the South according to geographic regions, the authors have been faced with the difficult task of making projections about clusters of states each of which tends to be characterized by striking ethnic, socioeconomic, and political heterogeneity. The authors have been faced also with the problem of discussing problems and interests that tend actually not to be confined to particular regions. Yet regional politics—its opportunities and constraints, its promises and threats—is likely to be increasingly important in the coming decade, confronting developing states in particular with a host of difficult choices. Rivalry for regional preeminence and disputes over territory and natural resources appear likely between or among states within all developing regions. At the same time, greater regional cooperation may increase the potential for accelerating national economic development, improving resource management, or inhibiting foreign intervention into domestic or regional affairs. While not all these matters are treated in depth in the following three essays, the authors suggest the goals that Southeast Asian states are

[2]The issue of relations between industrialized countries (the "North") and the developing countries (the "South") is one of central interest in the 1980s Project. Because this set of relations pervades so many issue areas, nearly all the work of the Project will take it into account. As well, a number of forthcoming volumes—on alternative goals and strategies—will deal directly with many aspects of the North-South relationship in the next decade and beyond.

likely to stress and the strategies they are most likely to adopt over the course of the next 10 to 15 years.

To be sure, writing comprehensively about Southeast Asia is very difficult. There is no conceptual tidiness possible when dealing with the richness of political and sociocultural diversity of the area. Yet as the authors of the following essays explain, this very diversity is one of several characteristics that clearly mark Southeast Asia and that may influence strongly the actions—domestic, regional, and international—of the Southeast Asian states over the next decade. Important also is the fact that more than any other region in the developing world, Southeast Asia has in recent years been "acted upon"—or permeated—by the currents of major power competition. The withdrawal of American armed forces from Indochina, the restoration of something approximating peace after a quarter-century of war, and the establishment of an apparently strong and unified Vietnam mark the beginning of a new era in Southeast Asia. But it is a beginning clouded by uncertainties about the future roles of foreign powers in the region and by the ideology and disproportionate power that have come to differentiate Vietnam from much of the rest of Southeast Asia. What is particularly interesting about the essays that follow is their interpretation from three different vantage points—political, economic, and sociocultural—of the implications posed by the region's permeability and diversity for national economic and political development, regional stability, and the solidarity of Southeast Asian states with the rest of the developing world.

In the first essay, Guy Pauker explores three political issues of central importance to the future of Southeast Asia: (1) the domestic political pressures in individual states likely to stem from and add to constraints on economic development, (2) the likely impact of two emerging centers of regional power—Vietnam and Indonesia—on regional stability or instability, and (3) the significance of the loosening of relations between Southeast Asian states and external powers. Pauker makes the important point that the Southeast Asian states—particularly the noncommunist states—are likely to have considerable difficulty in handling internal political problems despite their prospects for continued overall growth. As Pauker suggests, and Frank Golay's analysis

3

of future economic development confirms, domestic tensions may well grow as a result of the failure of development strategies to distribute evenly the benefits of economic growth to an increasing population.

According to Golay, Southeast Asian governments are likely to continue to pursue strategies of rapid industrialization dependent on protectionist policies even though such a development strategy has failed to expand economies quickly enough to absorb rapidly growing urban labor forces or to bolster dangerously low levels of subsistence in many rural areas. Additionally, in Southeast Asia as elsewhere in the Third World, governments will continue to try to limit the vulnerability of domestic economies to economic actions over which they have little control. One way Southeast Asian economies could accomplish this would be to close themselves off from the international economic system, as Burma has done and as Cambodia may do in the years ahead. But a strategy of isolation would be costly, and even Vietnam does not now appear eager to pursue it. The alternative—maintaining an open, though managed, economy—would confront Malaysia, Indonesia, the Philippines, and other Southeast Asian states with major problems such as escalating foreign exchange needs, increasing dependence on trade with Japan, and the threat to national economic sovereignty posed by extensive foreign investment.

While these problems of economic development are common to most states of the developing world, they are considerably complicated in Southeast Asia by the enormously diverse sociocultural makeup of societies in the region. According to Cynthia Enloe, the knotty ethnic problems that currently loom so large in Southeast Asian life are likely to persist through the 1980s—intensifying as governments seek to extend central authority and impinging on the ability of governments to translate their national goals into politically effective development programs. Efforts by groups to achieve "national" independence through secessionist movements (as in Burma or the Philippines) could lead to widespread armed violence or stimulate the use of repressive violence by leaders who feel that their positions are threatened by sporadic disorder. Where specific groups

4

monopolize positions of economic or political power (as in Thailand) they may profit disproportionately from development efforts at the expense of the rest of society or at the expense of a more optimal pattern of national development. Attempts by political leaders to expand their authority or to forge bonds of national unity (as in Vietnam and Indonesia) may threaten the identity and autonomy of minority groups and, when opposed, may lead to systematic and egregious violations of individual rights. Deliberate actions by those who have gained political power to wrest economic control or political influence from members of one cultural group or to shift the benefits of economic development from members of one group to members of another ethnic group (as in Malaysia) may cause distortions or bottlenecks in economic development (for example, by imposing political criteria on the location of industry or the allocation of government revenue). Under the circumstances, foreign governments may well bolster specific ethnic groups—deliberately or inadvertently—while seeking to bolster specific national governments or national development efforts, thereby contributing to an intensification of local ethnic differences.

The sociocultural and political divisiveness within the region is, moreover, likely to impede any significant advance in regional cooperation during the 1980s. As Golay's essay implies, the economic rationale for regional integration is not compelling enough to overcome the ethnic divisiveness and economic nationalism. And, as Enloe suggests, the problem of unequal gains among states which has plagued regional economic institutions in South and Central America is likely to be exacerbated in the Association of Southeast Asian Nations (ASEAN), where attempts by governments to deal with domestic distributional disputes among ethnic groups will make compromises on a regional level more difficult to attain. The flexibility of governments in regional negotiations, in other words, may well be constrained by governments' needs to accommodate communal pressures regarding such economic considerations as the location of industry, the allocation of resources to economic sectors, or the stipulations governing the operations of foreign enterprises.

As one reads Pauker's assessment of the political, diplomatic, and military trends in Southeast Asia, one is struck, however, by the extent to which changes in the international environment confront the Southeast Asian states with the necessity and opportunity to reexamine their foreign policy options in regard to both regional relations and relations with outside powers. As Pauker indicates, both the Southeast Asian governments and the extraregional powers that have been involved militarily within the region tend now to favor some "mutual disengagement" or loosening of special bilateral ties. While this loosening of bilateral relations may afford the Southeast Asian states greater room for maneuver in the future than they have experienced in the recent past, it also presents them with the need to work out a difficult balancing of diplomatic relations with the extraregional powers—the United States, the Soviet Union, Japan, China, and the European Economic Community—each of which is likely to continue to have interests of one kind or another in Southeast Asia that carry overtones of intervention.

At the same time, intraregional relations, vastly complicated by the special nature and great potential power of Vietnam, create tensions between aspirations for independence and the perceived need for recourse to outside support. As Pauker's paper makes clear, the combination of a cohesive leadership core, strong support from political cadres, well-developed methods of mobilization, and military forces equal to the total of those of all noncommunist states in the region gives Vietnam the capacity to pursue hegemonic aspirations, at least on the Indochinese peninsula, should it decide to do so. Vietnam's role therefore makes Southeast Asia unique among developing regions: only in that region might a state motivated by a revolutionary ideology assume a hegemonic role. The place of Vietnam in Southeast Asia is very different, for example, from that of Cuba in Latin America, Angola and Mozambique in Africa, or South Yemen in the Middle East. In other regions, the states that are militarily the strongest are today committed to the maintenance of the political status quo.

One can only speculate, however, about Hanoi's future behavior. Having achieved its aim of national unification and having helped purge its neighbors of hostile forces, the Vietnam leaders may now place the export of revolution very low on their list of priorities—considerably lower, for instance, than the reconstruction of their war-torn nation. One might argue, indeed, that Vietnam's leaders want most of all to see sturdily independent national regimes as their neighbors. Whether or not these are communist regimes is a matter of interest, but not necessarily of action, for Hanoi. On the other hand, even if the Vietnamese leadership were willing to "leave its neighbors alone," it might fail to keep that resolve. There are insurgent movements, more or less communist in orientation, in most of the other states of Southeast Asia. Each of these movements will look to Hanoi for moral support and material assistance. Given their own 30 years of revolutionary struggle, the Vietnamese leadership might well find it difficult not to support national liberation movements in neighboring states, especially if encouraged by a Soviet Union that saw opportunity in Southeast Asian turmoil. Moreover, such support would be almost costless for Hanoi. After all, the war made Vietnam a dumping ground for weapons; Hanoi's stock of light infantry weapons, the sort which insurgents would need, must be gigantic. Conversely, Vietnam needs so little from its neighbors that it is difficult to imagine they have any levers that could effectively be used to dissuade the Vietnamese from supporting insurgencies in neighboring countries. And no state or alliance of regional states is likely to have the power to oppose or to threaten Vietnam.

The one other state in the region that might appear to have the potential to rival Vietnam is Indonesia. But Indonesia, as Pauker asserts, is not likely to opt for a rival hegemonic role. It lacks the kind of internal political discipline that would support a reallocation of scarce resources away from economic development toward regional domination. And there is little likelihood of substantial outside support for a build-up of military force in Indonesia as a counterweight to Vietnam. Nor is Indonesia likely to forge an alliance with other ASEAN states oriented against Vietnam. Were the noncommunist states of Southeast Asia to organize against Vietnam, they could create an "unfriendly" environment that Hanoi would probably find politically unsettling but not one that would be seriously threatening. What is more, the construction of some sort of intraregional balance of power—especially one based on a confrontation between an increasingly solid communist group and the noncommunist states—would run the risk of stimulating the kind of arms race that incites escalation and tempts the kind of rival superpower intervention that the Southeast Asian states seem eager to avoid.

Ironically enough, what Hanoi is most likely to ask of its neighbors—a further attenuation of their relations with extraregional powers—is just what they are least likely to grant if Vietnam demonstrates resolve to dominate or destabilize political affairs in the region. It might be argued that the Vietnamese leadership could never really feel secure if Thailand were to reestablish close military relationships with the United States or if Indonesia or the Philippines were to acquire outside support for a substantial military build-up. Yet at a time when each, in varying degrees, is threatened by insurgent movements, and when the other states of the region seem weak reeds upon which to lean, a foreign connection may seem particularly valuable. This puts the other states of the region in a difficult dilemma: if they maintain a distance from extraregional powers, Hanoi may be less likely to support movements which threaten them; yet there is always the risk that appeals for revolutionary solidarity will be too compelling for the revolutionary leadership in Hanoi to resist. Uncertainty regarding the future roles of external powers complicates calculations of all the states in the region. Clearly the United States will be unlikely, for the foreseeable future, to consent to play a major military role in Southeast Asia. Yet furnishing military equipment and training need not constitute a major role. And this is precisely what might be sufficient to enable regimes like those of Thailand, Indonesia, and the Philippines to stave off insurgent threats.

The Soviet role is more problematic. In recent years Hanoi has clearly been closer to Moscow than to Peking. Certainly the Soviet Union can contribute more to Vietnam's reconstruction than can China. Yet at the same time, the Vietnamese leadership must surely be reluctant to intensify its dependence upon Moscow. Significant assistance by Vietnam to insurgent movements in Southeast Asia would inevitably require Soviet support—if only in the form of reinsurance against the risk of a significant

8

American reaction. Yet the stock of war material in Vietnam is so large and the threat of American reaction is so remote that Hanoi might be able to play an active revolutionary role without increasing its dependence on Moscow.

China, for its part, is unlikely to wish to see substantial intervention by Hanoi—and (at least in the eyes of Peking) an extension of Soviet influence—in the region. But whether the People's Republic would be able to take any significant steps either to dissuade Hanoi or, conversely, to strengthen the hands of other governments in the region is doubtful, especially since Chinese intimidation would likely force Hanoi deeper into the Soviet embrace and perhaps even increase Soviet military presence in Southeast Asia. As for Japan, its role throughout the period with which we are concerned will almost surely be confined to an extensive, but not deeply rooted, economic involvement. A more assertive political involvement on its part would be extremely unlikely—and military involvement would be altogether out of the question. Thus, Hanoi is likely to retain great freedom of action, with few disincentives to threatening the governments of its neighbors.

Perhaps as Vietnam seeks to expand its economic links with outside powers—especially the United States and Japan—those states will choose to link increased economic interaction with Vietnam to its performance in the region. But the other states of Southeast Asia have good reason to doubt that outside powers will act on their behalf. And they have good reason to be wary of the cost to national autonomy of continued dependence on extraregional powers for regional stability. Thus, the states of the region are faced, it would seem, with the need to devise among themselves ways to prevent interventionary or destabilizing behavior within the region. And, under these circumstances, greater regional cooperation, however difficult, would seem to offer the best chance for the states of the region to gain the ends they seek—greater autonomy, reduced dependence on and vulnerability to outside powers, regional stability, and resilient development.

In particular, regional cooperation would seem to offer a way to reconcile the desire for diversified political and economic relationships that promise greater freedom of action with national security concerns without incurring detrimental costs of competition for arms, for allies, and for aid. The member states of ASEAN have already declared their intent to establish Southeast Asia as a "zone of peace, friendship and neutrality." To gain Vietnam's de facto acceptance of this declared objective is undoubtedly of prime importance for the prospects of regional stability. A coordinated effort among ASEAN states in this regard would likely give each of them a sense of enhanced relative power—however short of far-reaching regional integration their cooperation falls. Should Vietnam demonstrate a willingness to normalize relations with other states in the region, then in the continuing process of diversifying and loosening relations with outside powers that may appear threatening to Vietnam, these states might begin to move to establish with Vietnam some mechanism for the exchange of views on security concerns and for the exchange of information on the local activities of extraregional powers. Clearly, such steps are not likely to occur in a brief span of time; but moves in these directions might contribute to the creation of "breathing space" in a region within which states have had little room to maneuver in the recent past. And these steps might enable Southeast Asian governments to avoid an arms race instigated by misperceptions of each other's aims. A less confrontational regional environment might also allow for a relaxation of internal security measures in ethnically divided societies—seen as too risky in a less secure setting—and even a search for long-range accommodation among domestic groups. It might also establish a climate within which the ASEAN states together with Vietnam could act to resolve growing disputes over claims to control of the resources of the surrounding seas and control of important regional straits.

There is not a great deal that extraregional powers can do to promote regional cooperation. But they can do quite a lot to avoid making it more difficult. By deed if not by explicit agreement, they can avoid making Southeast Asia an arena of competition, they can eschew preferential arrangements and bilateral security guarantees, and they can maintain normal relations with all states in the region regardless of ideological orientation. And where regional arrangements do exist, they can frequently add to their standing and prestige by dealing with them and by listening to their advice.

There is, of course, no certain connection between greater regional cooperation and faster economic development. Nor do economic development and a greater sense of security necessarily translate into increased national attention to problems of poverty, equity, and justice. Other volumes in the 1980s Project will directly address these problems. This one, as has been indicated, is designed to give a better sense of the particular problems confronting countries in one part of the world and to give an impression of the mosaic of conflicting needs, desires, and aspirations that is too often blurred by the all-embracing but not very informative or accurate portmanteau terms "Third World" and "less developed countries."

National Politics and Regional Powers

Guy J. Pauker

Introduction

The 10 countries of Southeast Asia—Brunei, Burma, Indonesia, Cambodia, Laos, Malaysia, Philippines, Singapore, Thailand, and Vietnam—constitute a complex and colorful cluster of ethnic entities whose people have been exposed to the influence of all major world cultures and religions. Penetration of the area by outsiders was facilitated by its geographic location along the sea lanes between the Indian Ocean and the Pacific, and at the crossroads of Asia's two high cultures, India and China, and, curiously, by the attraction that tropical spices exerted on early Muslim and Christian merchant navigators.

For three centuries only coastal points on some of the islands which are now part of Indonesia and the Philippines were of interest to Spanish and Portuguese adventurers, followed shortly by British and Dutch competitors. Only in the nineteenth century did colonialism begin to penetrate more deeply into the life of those islands. Then, the growing Franco-British imperialist rivalry prompted the exploration and conquest of Burma and Vietnam on the mainland, while the Thais in the middle were anxiously striving to understand the West so as to be able to ward off its encroachments.

Although some territories changed hands—Indonesia for a few years from Dutch to British control, the Philippines for half a century when the United States took over from Spain—Southeast Asia was not an area of intense geopolitical concern until Japan, seeking secure access to natural resources, occupied the whole region, taking advantage of the major colonial powers' misfortunes in the early phase of World War II. Three years of Japanese military occupation created favorable conditions for the rapid growth of the already budding nationalist movements and set in motion the process of decolonization.

Strategic interests, economic expectations, or cultural attraction cannot explain the attention Southeast Asia received after 1945. An area that should have been known primarily through the novels of Joseph Conrad or Somerset Maugham became in strange ways a major obsession for American policy makers. A widely shared but never justified assumption that Southeast Asia had major strategic significance dominated American collective perceptions through two Republican and two Democratic administrations, from Eisenhower's "domino theory" and Southeast Asia Treaty Organization, through Kennedy's preoccupation with Laos and Johnson's sacrifice of his vision of a "Great Society" for a $150 billion war in Vietnam, to the final ignominy of Nixon's invasion of neutral Cambodia.

In retrospect, it seems obvious that the "domino" which really mattered had fallen in 1949 when the Kuomintang lost China to the Communist party and that by comparison with that historic event it was strategically insignificant whether the area controlled by Vietnamese Communists extended to the 13th or stopped at the 17th parallel North, or whether Laos and Cambodia tilted East rather than West. Geographic location, political structure, human resources, and nature's bounty did not justify, without Procrustean distortion, arguments concerning Southeast Asia's vital importance to the United States.

Early American support of the region's nationalist aspirations could have spared later ordeals which retarded the historical process without significantly deflecting its course. After they had been driven out by Japan's Imperial Army, the colonial powers were in no position to reverse the nationalist awakening and social mobilization which had occurred in Southeast Asia since the turn of the century, inspired in part by the Meiji Restoration and by Japan's spectacular victory against Imperial Russia in 1904–1905.

The intensity of the struggle against colonialism did not increase the intrinsic importance of the region for the rest of humanity any more than a similar historical process occurring a century earlier in Central and Eastern Europe enhanced the contribution of the Balkans to the destiny of humanity, except as a transitory source of conflict among the great powers of that period. The unrealistic geopolitical enlargement of the region's image was the result of American misconceptions which cannot be ascribed exclusively to the trauma caused by the communist victory in China and to the outrage generated by the Korean War. A full explanation is still lacking.

Thirty years after the end of World War II, the age of Western dominance in Southeast Asia was brought to a close by the communist victories in Indochina. The industrial democracies— the United States, the European Economic Community, and Japan—will without doubt avoid future political-military entanglements in the region, despite their continued interest in business on commercial terms. As a consequence, in the coming decade Southeast Asia might enjoy considerable freedom from external pressures and interventions, unless it becomes the arena of intensified strategic maneuvers in the setting of the Sino-Soviet conflict.

China has an obvious interest in seeing Southeast Asia remain weak and divided, so as to minimize the possibility of military threats on its southern borders, whereas the Soviet Union could become actively interested in helping the development and regional integration of Southeast Asia in the hope of forging an alliance capable of keeping China at bay both in the north and in the south.

ONE

Geographic Abstraction or Political Reality?

Located between India and China, Asia's two major centers of gravity, Southeast Asia can be misconstrued as a comparably cohesive entity, when in fact it is the cultural fringes of those two great Asian civilizations where for centuries countless tribes were able to survive without being absorbed and assimilated by either empire. After the Portuguese conquered Malacca in 1511, Western imperialism penetrated the region slowly and became an unintentional barrier against the expansionist proclivities of both Indians and Chinese and a buffer preventing a direct political collision between them.[1]

Indian cultural influences decisively penetrated Burma, Thailand, Laos, Cambodia, and parts of Malaysia and Indonesia. Chinese culture had a similarly strong impact on Vietnam, while leaving numerous traces in those parts of Indonesia, Malaysia, and the Philippines where Hindu-Buddhist influences were less intense. The non-Asian powers which established their dominion in the region during the short-lived age of Western imperialism had a more limited direct cultural impact on the masses. But they shaped the outlook of the elites and played a decisive role in delineating the boundaries of the colonies which emerged after World War II as independent states claiming national status.

[1]This perspective on the history of Southeast Asia was given by Prime Minister J. Nehru to a group of Americans at the end of the April 1955 Asian-African Conference in Bandung, during an interview in the presence of his daughter, Indira Gandhi.

19

None of the independent states of Southeast Asia has yet developed national cohesion to go with its sovereign status, however, and the fragility of national identities is a major source of self-doubt among the elites and accounts for their present intransigent nationalism. In the absence of strong national entities in Southeast Asia, regional collective action—which presupposes some compromise of national autonomy—is not likely over the course of the next 15 years. The national integrity of these immature political entities is also threatened by centrifugal forces driven directly or indirectly by ethnic pluralism, described so well by Cynthia Enloe.[2] Even older European nations and the miraculous American melting pot are experiencing the corrosive impact of ethnic divisiveness. In Southeast Asia, where tribal and linguistic pluralisms are still the dominant reality of daily life rather than the somewhat artificial construct of small numbers of marginal people, the retardation of national crystallization is bound to have very major domestic and regional (and perhaps even international) consequences, inviting repressive policies within each state and tempting neighbors and external powers to intervene.

The generation of Southeast Asians born after World War II, the first educated under the myths and symbols of the new nations, will seek to control the destinies of their countries in the decades ahead. Lacking the self-confidence of well-established nations with a historically tested capacity for survival, a cultural heritage valid in terms of contemporary rather than folkloristic-antiquarian values, a scientific and technological substratum from which a modern industrial economy can grow without excessive dependence on external sustenance, common values and interests, collective memories, and institutional traditions, the governments of Southeast Asia will find it difficult to play a predictable and significant role in world and regional affairs. At present the positions taken by these governments on domestic and international matters are still too often the result of the individual whims and preferences of those in authority and lack the firm foundation provided by the instincts and views of a broad-based and well-nurtured public opinion.

[2]Cynthia Enloe, "Ethnic Diversity: The Potential for Conflict," pp. 135–181 in this volume.

The lack of continuity in the historical tradition of Southeast Asia, caused by the interposition of a period of colonial tutelage, can only be remedied by the passage of time. Tribal groups and historical kingdoms collided, fought, pillaged, and conquered as far back as can be ascertained through written records and archaeological evidence. Then, armed violence between indigenous organized social groups was drastically curtailed by the superior military power of the colonial rulers, who were constantly engaged in repressive campaigns for the establishment or protection of their own versions of law and order. As a result, population increased while nascent native administrative and political skills atrophied. Deprived of the opportunity to make their own decisions, most countries of Southeast Asia were slow to develop leaders, managers, and administrators, as well as organizational skills and habits in the public and the private sector alike. Even in Vietnam and Singapore it remains to be seen whether the first generation of truly able leaders was a historical accident or the result of advanced political development.

The withdrawal of external military power in the course of emancipation from colonial rule after World War II was accompanied by a resurgence of civil strife within the newly independent states. In a number of instances, domestic political violence was aided and abetted by external powers. The outstanding example was the war in Indochina. But whereas violence became endemic and epidemic within the Southeast Asian states, the instances of armed conflict among neighbors have been few in number and limited in scope. The protracted operations of Communist Vietnamese forces in Laos is the most prominent instance of war among neighbors in the contemporary history of Southeast Asia.

Another notable instance of aggression against a neighbor was Sukarno's "confrontation" with Malaysia from 1963 to 1966, which was constrained by the reluctance of the Indonesian Army to get too deeply involved in military operations abroad while the Communist Party of Indonesia was advancing successfully on the road to power and by the forbidding presence of British strike forces in Malaysia and Singapore.

Overt and covert military operations by Indonesia in Western New Guinea in 1962–1963 while it was still under Dutch occupation, and in Timor in 1975–1976 in the twilight of Portuguese decolonization, are less easy to appraise without a lengthy discussion about the role of violence in the struggle against colonialism.

Given the intense nationalism of the new elites of Southeast Asia, the relative absence of armed clashes between neighboring countries is quite remarkable. All countries in the region control territories which could become the object of some neighbor's irredentist claim on ethnic or historical grounds. The borders of Southeast Asia are the product of alien interference and are too new to have been legitimized by the passage of time. Does the fact that most governments have abstained from pursuing territorial claims indicate self-restraint or weakness? Obviously, challenging the territorial order of the colonial period would open a Pandora's box, to the eventual detriment of all concerned. But such self-restraint may also reflect the weakness of the states established after World War II. None of the governments of Southeast Asia had until now the capacity to engage in external military adventures against relatively equal adversaries unless they were assured of external logistic support. Sukarno's "confrontation" with Malaysia and Vietnamese operations in Laos both relied on logistic support from communist countries.

The Vietnamese armed conflict between 1959 and 1975, the outstanding example of a civil war supported by external powers, could not have attained such scope and duration had only domestic resources been used. While some insurgencies in the region did receive external logistic support, the policy of the United States has been to prohibit offensive operations across national borders by the recipients of American military assistance. As the result of these safeguards, neither North Vietnam nor North Korea were invaded by the armed forces of South Vietnam and South Korea, which were trained, equipped, and supplied by the United States for defensive operations only.

It is an interesting question whether the Philippines would have pursued a more aggressive course of action in support of its claim to the Sabah territories of Malaysia if its logistic support came from a great power with a less restrictive policy of military assistance than the United States. Despite the strong American interest in the Philippine bases and the lack of any American defense commitment to Malaysia, the question whether the United

States should support the forceful "liberation" of Sabah was never raised.

Aside from the struggle in Indochina, the governments and peoples of Southeast Asia have not fought each other often enough to get to know each other as adversaries, nor learned to work together through joint ventures in war and peace. In contrast, European cooperation was preceded by centuries of conflict during which Europeans came to recognize some common interests. In the precolonial period in Southeast Asia there was warfare between Burmese, Thai, Cambodians, Vietnamese, and others, usually followed by territorial annexations. Then Western colonialism stabilized the relations between neighboring countries and froze the map of Southeast Asia. Accordingly, Southeast Asia is still essentially a geographic abstraction, for its peoples are still quite far from recognizing an interest in pursuing some common goals through regional cooperation or collective action.

Because of infrequent contacts between neighboring states, even the elites and certainly the masses, unlike the nations of Europe, have limited knowledge of each other. To this day, a generation after independence, the elites are often more familiar with current events in the homelands of their former colonial overlords than with the problems of their immediate neighbors, in part because of the nature of international news coverage. In the absence of a feeling of community between peoples, regional initiatives by governments are not likely to have a substantive impact.

Southeast Asia remains compartmentalized by great ethnic and linguistic diversity, the lack of a shared sense of history, and the experience of different colonial administrations; it is characterized by religious pluralism, lack of economic complementarity, ideological cleavage, and political controversy about the source and nature of external threats. Given these conditions, it is unlikely that by the end of the next decade Southeast Asia will have become a community of countries capable of coordinating their political, economic, and security interests and speaking with one voice in world affairs.

TWO

Society, Polity, and Development in Southeast Asia

The modern nation-states of Southeast Asia commenced their existence under the aegis of constitutions which were expected to give the people the benefit of representative political institutions and of the rule of law; but the attempt to establish the rule of law in Southeast Asia has not been successful. All governments of Southeast Asia have reverted to authoritarianism when their capacity for crisis management failed to overcome personal ambitions, group selfishness, social conflicts, or economic crises, and the unfamiliar rules of the political game imported from the West proved unworkable.

Human rights are in jeopardy everywhere in the area, while military or quasi-military organizations in control of the state's means of coercion provide an alternative power base for governments lacking electorally validated popular consent and operating outside the constraints of the rule of law. Western-style procedural safeguards have been discarded whenever they conflicted with the requirement of protecting the position of those in power. The rules of governmental succession remain unpredictable, with incumbents and challengers equally devoid of hereditary or elective legitimacy.

In daily practice, these issues are, of course, not as significant to the people as they are to political philosophers. The masses judge governments on pragmatic grounds. If times are good, the ruler is viewed as the legitimate holder of a "heavenly mandate" and the procedures by which power was acquired become retroactively legitimized. But in most of Southeast Asia today times are not good, raising the question of what forms of government will eventually emerge from the historical crucible after traditional forms of government, democratic-constitutional institutions, and the authoritarian rule of the military will all have failed the pragmatic tests of problem solving.

The only exception is the remarkable city-state of Singapore, governed by a team of fanatically honest and exceptionally competent civilian leaders who have been able to achieve high rates of economic growth as well as visible social progress and distributive justice, while using emergency measures sparingly against extraparliamentary opposition. But even this first-generation success story has still to face the test of successful transfer of power to an equally virtuous and talented second generation of leaders.

The communist rulers of Vietnam can also be singled out as a special case. The same group has governed liberated areas from jungle hideouts from 1945 to 1954, North Vietnam from Hanoi after their victory against France, and the whole country since the collapse of the American-supported regime in Saigon. Throughout these three decades, Ho Chi Minh's comrades have maintained a solidarity unequaled by any other political team, while all other Communist parties have been ravaged by factional strife. Whether this unique achievement has also generated good government for the Vietnamese people is difficult to establish yet, both because of the harsh controls exerted by the regime in all areas under its authority and because of the gigantic burdens shouldered by that nation during 30 years of unrelenting political and military warfare.

POLITICAL DISSATISFACTION AND
STUDENT UNREST

In most of the other states of Southeast Asia, however, political leadership has not been exceptional, nor have economic conditions been favorable. General dissatisfaction has been growing, and in the last few years most Southeast Asian governments have been challenged by increasingly militant and highly politicized student movements which are likely to be the principal threat to political stability in the coming decade. Labor and farmers are easily controlled; their organizations are repressed or manipulated by the respective governments. Students live in an environment which governments cannot as easily control. Their repression is rendered more difficult by the fact that many students are the children of the ruling elites. The events of the last two or three years are indicative of the political difficulties the noncommunist governments of Southeast Asia will face in the coming decade.

In Burma, higher education virtually ceased in 1975 following student riots and demonstrations protesting rampant inflation and rising unemployment. In Thailand, the student riots of October 1973 brought down the military government of Field Marshal Thanom Kittikachorn, after which student activism prevented civilian governments from functioning effectively until October 1976 when clashes between left-wing and right-wing students, manipulated by various shadowy forces, culminated in a ghastly outburst of violence at Thammasat University in Bangkok. At that point the military, which had obviously been waiting for the right moment and had allegedly made careful preparations for such an occasion as early as January 1976, acted swiftly. The constitution was abolished, all civilian courts were placed under military jurisdiction, communism was outlawed, and newspapers were temporarily banned and then placed under strict controls, "in order not to let Thailand become a prey to the communists and to uphold the monarchy and the royal family." Two days later a supreme court justice, Mr. Thanin Kraivichien, who had been severely critical of the democratic governments of the last three years, was appointed prime minister and the new government immediately showed a firm hand by issuing a large number of decrees, in contrast with the abolished National Assembly, which had adopted only two bills in the last five months.[3]

[3]All major newspapers covered these events in their October 7, 1976, issues and during the next few days, but the *Washington Post* published in addition a full page of United Press International photos documenting the inhuman brutality of the clashes between left-wing and right-wing students, the latter supported by armed police and the military.

In the Philippines, student activism has been repressed since the proclamation of martial law by President Ferdinand Marcos in September 1972. In Malaysia, according to Professor R. S. Milne of the University of British Columbia, "in 1974 the two greatest challenges to governmental authority came from students and from communist activity." In 1975 the campuses were quiet, but the government amended the Universities and University Colleges Act so as to ensure greater control over students, who were prohibited from becoming members of, or supporting, parties, trade unions, or other bodies without university approval. Even Singapore had student demonstrations in 1974, and in February 1975 the University of Singapore Students' Union president was jailed for a year for inciting a riot on trade union premises.[4]

In Indonesia, the present regime under General Suharto was established 10 years ago with substantial assistance from student activists, who demonstrated and rioted against the corrupt and incompetent government of the late President Sukarno. The students then became increasingly alienated from the new national leaders, whom they criticized for corruption, extravagance, and lack of concern for social justice. In January 1974, during the visit of Japanese Prime Minister Tanaka, feelings exploded in numerous acts of vandalism and arson. The tension has not yet subsided.

Active literacy is still very low in Southeast Asia. The media of mass communication are controlled by the government and reach only a small fraction of the total population; consequently, students are a relatively more important segment of public opinion than they are in industrial democracies. The vast majority of students come from the middle classes, because higher education is still beyond the reach of most children of poor farmers and workers. But even for middle-class families, providing means for the higher education of their children in most cases entails considerable sacrifice and, to a much greater extent than in the West, is viewed as an investment which should in time benefit the whole family. Yet unemployment, underemployment, or at least very

[4]R. S. Milne, "Malaysia and Singapore, 1975," *Asian Survey*, February 1976, pp. 190, 192.

inadequate compensation is the fate of most graduates, especially as career choices do not take fully into account demand and supply for various specialties in the job market. Because the countries of Southeast Asia entered the process of economic growth only recently, the base to which growth rates apply is narrow and the results are modest in quantitative terms, even under favorable circumstances. The developmental process does not create enough jobs of any kind, not to mention meaningful and rewarding ones, to absorb the graduates of high schools and universities.

This fact is bound to have a decisive impact on the future political dynamics of Southeast Asia. The alienation of youth in all the noncommunist countries is a portent of stormy years ahead. In the period between World Wars I and II, uprooted young Europeans who were trying to escape the poverty and hopelessness of their social background through higher education, but found their way blocked by economic depression, turned murderously against the established order and became easy recruits of extremist movements. More recently, in the United States, Western Europe, and Japan, alienated activists have turned to anarchistic terrorism. Such fanaticism, now as then, tends to polarize politics, reducing governmental ability to cope with the problems which led to alienation in the first place.

The viciousness of clashes between left- and right-wing students in Bangkok in October 1976, which included lynchings and other inhumanities, is a disturbing symptom that explosive social tensions are building up among some members of the younger generation in Southeast Asia. It is likely that this potential for violence can and will be exploited by a large number of interested parties, including politicians in need of muddy waters, ideological groups manipulating the political process, and foreign agents involved in the maneuvers of regional and global power politics.

Needless to say, students are only a small fraction of the total population of Southeast Asia, and in many respects a privileged one. Their activism reflects the fact that they are among the most energetic elements of society. Their social awareness and political consciousness makes them particularly sensitive to the deficiencies of the prevailing systems of government and impatient for remedies.

29

Although until now overt symptoms of alienation have appeared only in Southeast Asia's civilian intellectuals, it is possible that as dissatisfaction with present conditions mounts, military officers of the same generation, sharing the social and cultural background of unversity students, will join in active opposition to the present regimes, in which case resort to violence is likely to increase.

POPULATION AND EMPLOYMENT

An increasingly large segment of the total Southeast Asian population consists of young adults without higher education. Statistics vary, but it is a known fact that economic development in Southeast Asia is not progressing fast enough to provide full employment for the rapidly growing numbers of young adults. The problem will get worse because the population of Southeast Asia is young. An estimated 43 percent were under 15 years of age in 1976, whereas in the United States only 27 percent were in the same age group, and in Europe only 24 percent. The implications in terms of demand for employment, housing, education, recreational activities, and social services are staggering.

The 1971 census of Indonesia "confirms other evidence showing that unemployment is concentrated in the younger age groups and is higher among the better educated."[5] The social mobilization of the unemployed is bound to increase in the next 15 years and their political consciousness will broaden, despite governmental efforts to damp these processes. They are a political factor of immense potential significance.

Although Southeast Asia's poor seem still to accept their fate with resignation and governments have acquired considerable skills in security operations, it is likely that mass education and the gradual diffusion of public information through electronic channels and urbanization will generate growing opposition to corrupt elites. At the same time, understanding of political processes and therefore of citizen ability to apply pressure to government decision making will also be growing.

[5]H. W. Arndt, "Development and Equality: The Indonesian Case," *World Development,* February–March 1975, p. 82.

How long it will take until a "critical mass" is reached in each country cannot be predicted. Specific domestic conditions are usually of primary importance, but the demonstration effect of unrest in one country can become the catalyst for similar unrest in another. Only a massive resurgence of hope in the future and of confidence in the capacity of governments to achieve significant progress can reverse current trends. Otherwise, present prospects for peaceful growth are not promising.

It was apparent 20 years ago that systemic changes were needed in Southeast Asia, and there has been no lack of turmoil since then. Convulsions have occurred within the framework of the present social order, and it is not clear what alternatives the historical process will generate and when this might happen. A few facts and figures about present conditions in the countries of Southeast Asia will broaden the reader's perspective.

Table 1 offers an overview of population growth in Southeast Asia, based on the most recent United Nations calculations which use a "medium variant" concerning annual rates of growth. The purpose of presenting these figures is to give some indication of the task facing the respective governments in the next 15 years.

A reliable comparison of present and future potential labor forces in Southeast Asia would require statistical data which are not available. But using some of the macro-assumptions made by Georges Tapinos for the 1980s Project, one can speculate that by 1990 the total population in Southeast Asia in the 15–64 age group—persons already born—is likely to increase by a total of 90 million. The interpretation of trends in developing countries concerning the participation rate of women in the labor force is a controversial issue.[6] One does not know how many women in the 15–64 age group will seek jobs. This will have a major impact on the total size of the labor force, besides other factors such as the extension of education beyond the age of 18 and the frequency of retirement before the age of 65. As none of these conditions can be anticipated accurately, one can only assume that jobs will be needed for more than half of the 90 million persons who will enter

[6]Georges Tapinos, "The World in the 1980s: Demographic Perspectives," working title of a 1980s Project Volume, McGraw-Hill, New York, forthcoming.

TABLE 1
Projected Population (thousands)

	1975	1980	1985	1990
Southeast Asia	323,838	370,854	423,242	478,712
Brunei	147	160	175	189
Burma	31,240	35,195	39,687	44,573
Cambodia	8,110	9,409	10,911	12,491
Indonesia*	136,716	155,624	176,317	197,519
Laos	3,303	3,721	4,182	4,678
Malaysia	12,093	13,998	16,076	18,260
Philippines	44,437	52,203	60,862	70,119
Singapore	2,248	2,437	2,636	2,829
Thailand	42,093	49,473	57,784	66,752
Vietnam	43,451	48,634	54,612	61,302

SOURCE: United Nations, *World Population Prospects 1970–2000, as Assessed in 1973,* quoted in Georges Tapinos, "The World in the 1980s: Demographic Perspectives," McGraw-Hill, New York, forthcoming.
*Projections for Indonesia include East Timor.

the labor force between now and 1990. Providing these jobs will present a task of staggering proportions for governments which are by and large not distinguished for their management skills and which will be unable to mobilize the capital needed for the creation of jobs.

Cultivable land is becoming scarce everywhere in Southeast Asia, but food production can still be increased very substantially by intensive, scientific agriculture. In the coming decade, despite rapid population increases, Southeast Asia is not likely to become a food-deficit area, although the distribution of food between exporting countries like Thailand and importing countries like Indonesia might create occasional balance-of-payments problems. The most difficult question is how to achieve a satisfactory distribution of food within each country, in the absence of welfare policies or other means of income distribution, which would give the poorest elements in those societies access to their share of the available food. The absorption of large numbers of landless rural laborers into agricultural production—even if it were economi-

32

cally desirable to make it more labor-intensive—would require new forms of social organization, incompatible with the prevailing pattern of small, private land holdings. To open new lands by clearing forests would require inputs of capital and organizational skills which are both very scarce. Even countries like Thailand begin to experience the pressure of population on land.

The forced migration inflicted on the Cambodians after April 1975, when the whole population of Phnom Penh was driven at gunpoint into the countryside, is certainly not a desirable model. Alternatively, the Indonesian government's very small "transmigration" program, aimed at voluntarily moving several thousand families annually from Java to the Outer Islands, is still too modest to contribute significantly to the solution of Indonesia's population problems.

Population movements do occur spontaneously in Java as well as in less overcrowded areas of Southeast Asia, not from overpopulated villages into the wilderness but from the countryside to the cities. The noncommunist countries use only mild administrative measures to slow down this flow. The landless and unemployed poor seek relief in the urban environment, although in most Southeast Asian countries public welfare is not available. How they survive in the increasingly overcrowded cities—20 percent of the Southeast Asian population is urban—is not well understood either by government officials or by researchers. They saturate the carrying capacity of public utilities, create abominable slum conditions, and introduce an explosive mixture of frustration and resentment into the economic growth centers of the new states.

ECONOMIC DEVELOPMENT

Obviously, rapid growth of industry and services is required to absorb the growing labor forces of Southeast Asia which even intensive agricultural development will not fully utilize. But a favorable balance between the growth rate of the GNP and the population growth rate of a given state does not indicate whether the whole new labor force is productively integrated into the economic system. It only shows that the production of goods and services is increasing on a per capita basis, without giving any information about actual distribution. Positive growth rates are a necessary though not a sufficient condition of social welfare. Recent efforts to develop a composite measure to estimate whether basic human needs are equitably met have produced a new concept, the "Physical Quality of Life Index" (PQLI), based on life expectancy, infant mortality, and literacy. It suggests that Sri Lanka, with an average per capita GNP of 130, can have a PQLI of 83, while Malaysia, with an average per capita GNP of 680, may have a PQLI of 59.[7] For developing countries, which are heavily dependent on exports for revenue and on imports for capital goods, foreign trade is another important indicator of their prospects for economic growth. Some relevant economic data, collected by the United States government, are presented in Table 2.

TABLE 2
National Income and Foreign Trade

	GNP/GDP* ($ millions)	Per capita ($)	Exports ($ millions)	Imports ($ millions)
Brunei	177 (GNP) (1971)	1,430 (1971)	199 (1974)	125 (1974)
Burma	2,900 (GDP) (1975)	96 (1975)	210 (1974)	125 (1974)
Cambodia	950 (GNP) (1971)	140 (1971)	15 (1974)	210 (1974)
Indonesia	20,000 (GDP) (1974)	150 (1974)	7,426 (1974)	3,842 (1974)
Laos	220 (GNP) (1972)	70 (1972)	10 (1973)	62 (1973)
Malaysia	8,700 (GNP) (1974)	715 (1974)	5,000 (1974)	4,400 (1974)
Philippines	14,000 (GNP) (1974)	340 (1974)	2,625 (1974)	3,140 (1974)
Singapore	5,500 (GNP) (1974)	2,400 (1974)	6,200 (1974)	8,900 (1974)
Thailand	12,200 (GDP) (1974)	280 (1974)	2,477 (1974)	3,168 (1974)

*GDP equals GNP plus income earned in country but sent abroad, minus income earned abroad but sent into country. GDP exceeds GNP in debtor countries, reverse in creditor countries.

SOURCE: Central Intelligence Agency, *National Basic Intelligence Factbook*, January 1976. For Vietnam, available data are obsolete.

[7]John W. Sewell et al., *The United States and World Development: Agenda 1977*, Praeger for the Overseas Development Council, New York, 1977, pp. 147–154.

The absolute poverty of Southeast Asia becomes evident when one attempts to estimate a total GNP for the region. Using the data in Table 2 and adding $47 million for East Timor, on the assumption that it is as poor as Laos, and $4.3 billion for Vietnam, assuming that it is as poor as Burma, the total GNP/GDP for Southeast Asia around 1974–1975 would have been about $69 billion. Spain, with a population of 36 million, or about one-tenth of that of Southeast Asia, had a GNP of $73.3 billion in 1974. Yet from the perspective of the advanced industrial democracies, Spain is one of the poorer Western countries.

The enormous spread in per capita GNP within the region raises some interesting and important questions: What accounts for a range of $70 to $2,400 (CIA figures), or from $60 to $1,830 (World Bank figures)? Are these disparities the result of differences in national character, economic system, prior history, terms of trade? These are unanswered questions well worth addressing.

The relative poverty of the region as a whole should also be noted. According to United States government calculations, the world gross national product for 1974 was $4,820 billion.[8] This means that Southeast Asia's $69 billion amounted to 1.43 percent of the total. In 1975 Southeast Asia had 8.1 percent of the total world population, which means that its per capita GNP was only between one-fifth and one-sixth of the world's average—a very poor region indeed.

It is unlikely that the present governments of the non-communist countries of Southeast Asia will be able to provide employment through normal market mechanisms for the tens of millions of persons who will join the labor force in the next 15 years. Neither capital nor management will be available on a scale commensurate with the demand for jobs, even if a labor-intensive mix of factors of production would be adopted. Mass mobilization public work schemes, comparable to the employment policies of

[8]Central Intelligence Agency, *Handbook of Economic Statistics, 1975,* Washington, D.C., August 1975.

the neighboring communist countries, might become unavoidable to provide the whole population with minimum means of subsistence. The contribution of such social welfare measures to the rate of economic growth of each state will, of course, depend on the quality of the state's economic planning and the direction of its development strategy.

Even those men and women who are gainfully employed will be increasingly frustrated by the dim prospects the future has in store for them. Except for Singapore, which achieved an average real growth rate of 12.3 percent between 1966 and 1974 but dropped to 6.8 percent in 1974, the other noncommunist countries of Southeast Asia, such as Burma, Indonesia, Thailand, and the Philippines, achieved respectable but not spectacular rates of growth which cannot work miracles in rapidly overcoming poverty.

According to the data of the CIA, which seem optimistic, average real rates of growth in 1974–1975 were 3.5 percent for Burma, 4.5 percent for Thailand, 5.8 percent for the Philippines, 6.0 percent for Malaysia, and 7.8 percent for Indonesia. Were these figures to remain constant, and accepting the per capita incomes recorded in Table 2 at face value, Burma's per capita income would double in 20 years, reaching $192 in 1995; Thailand's per capita income would double in 15.5 years, reaching $560 in 1991; the Philippines' per capita income would double in 12 years, reaching $680 in 1987; Malaysia's per capita income would double in 11 2/3 years, reaching $1,430 in 1987; and Indonesia's per capita income would double in less than 9 years, reaching $300 in 1984.

Actually, rates of growth are affected by too many imponderables to make meaningful 10- to 20-year projections. These figures are presented only to make the point that even optimistic assumptions do not promise Southeast Asia relief from economic problems, especially as an increasingly outward-looking, better educated population will be more subject to the psychological impact of "relative deprivation" than isolated and tradition-bound villages were.

The base to which the above-mentioned rates of growth apply makes a great difference. The prospect of $300 per capita in Indonesia in 1984 is much less satisfactory than the expectation of

$1,430 per capita in Malaysia in 1987. But the more difficult question is the much debated problem of whether growth in the Third World "trickles down" or whether the rich get richer while the poor get poorer.

According to estimates made in 1975, the lowest 40 percent of the Indonesian population received 15 percent of the national income. They had a per capita income of $48 per year, as against a national average per capita income of $128. Fifty million Indonesians were living on an income of 16 cents (U.S.) per person per day.[9]

Besides the problem of distribution or social justice, which has not yet been solved in the noncommunist countries of Southeast Asia, another issue likely to have an increasingly great impact on the political dynamics of those countries is the frustration and alienation that the educated are bound to experience as they become aware how modest the expectations are that they can realistically entertain and how far behind the affluent countries they will remain throughout their lifetime. Last year Indonesian students were asking in private discussions whether a real rate of growth of 10 percent, which would require great austerity in order to mobilize the resources needed for capital formation, was worth the trouble as it would only bring average annual per capita income to $300 after seven years. This pessimism is dangerously paralyzing, though understandable in states whose elites give the young generation a disastrous example of venality and self-indulgence.

The intensity of alienation among Southeast Asian students is not directly related to the economic performance of governments; Singapore students seem no less restless than their Burmese colleagues. The young generation in noncommunist Southeast Asia is buffeted between idealism and cynicism and could easily be influenced by puritan extremists like the Vietnamese Communists, offering austere devotion to a higher purpose, or by romantic nationalist demagogues promising thrills and glory. In any case, unless the present elites offer solutions to the deepening

[9]Sumitro Djojohadikusumo, *Indonesia toward the Year 2000*, Jakarta, February 1975, p. 35. (Mimeographed.)

socioeconomic crisis in the region within the setting of the present regimes, major political upheavals are likely to occur in Southeast Asia in the coming decade.

THREE

The Future Role of Great and Other Powers

Before the Japanese occupation of Southeast Asia at the beginning of 1942, the powers external to the region which shaped the destinies of the peoples of Southeast Asia were the United States, Great Britain, France, the Netherlands, and Portugal. Of these, only the United States still plays multiple roles in the area—political, military, economic, cultural—whereas the others have gradually retrenched their activities and presently maintain only normal economic and cultural relations. Japan has become a very important trading partner, as illustrated in Table 3, but avoids involvement in the political and military affairs of the region. Neither the Soviet Union nor the People's Republic of China is likely to displace the United States, Western Europe, and Japan as leading economic partners with Southeast Asia.

Under the security umbrella provided by the military presence of the United States during the last quarter of a century, the industrial democracies have retained a dominant influence in Southeast Asia. Indonesia, for instance, received $4.325 billion total gross official bilateral capital flows between 1954 and 1973 from the 16 members of the Development Assistance Committee of the Organization for Economic Cooperation and Development. Of this, $1.732 billion came from the United States. By contrast, from 1956 to 1966, when all aid from communist sources was stopped, Indonesia received only $114 million in economic aid from the Soviet Union, $105 million from the People's Repub-

TABLE 3
Trade of Southeast Asian Countries with Japan
as a Percentage of Their Total Trade, 1974
($ millions)

Country*	Exports Amounts	%	Imports Amounts	%	Total Amounts	%	Rank: Total Trade
Indonesia	3,954.80	53.26	1,139.23	30.35	5,094.00	45.56	1
Malaysia	713.92	16.90	915.46	22.00	1,629.38	19.43	1
North Vietnam	27.30	60.10	22.50	28.40	49.80	42.03	1
Philippines	932.40	34.90	923.90	26.90	1,856.30	30.40	2†
Singapore	637.60	11.00	1,528.50	18.20	2,166.10	15.27	1
Thailand	639.20	25.90	1,009.75	32.70	1,648.95	29.66	1

*Burma, Cambodia, Laos omitted because the amounts are insignificant.
†Virtually equal to the United States.
SOURCE: International Monetary Fund, *Direction of Trade, 1970–74.*

lic of China, and $263 million from Eastern European countries.[10] This represents 11.14 percent of the capital flow from the industrial democracies up to the present.

Soviet trade with Indonesia started to increase again only in the last three years. Soviet exports rose from $3.6 million in 1973 to $10.6 million in 1974 and Soviet imports from $5.7 million in 1973 to $26.3 million in 1974. The total volume of $36.9 million must be viewed against the Japanese total of $5.094 billion during the same calendar year. Total trade with the Soviet Union amounted in 1974 to 0.72 percent of total trade with Japan.

Until now the contribution of communist countries to the economic development of Indonesia has been very small, and the fact that transactions with the Soviet Union are even mentioned in the Indonesian press is due to a certain eagerness in Jakarta to maintain an image of nonalignment or equidistance—to use a term which has become fashionable in Southeast Asian circles. Some

[10]Central Intelligence Agency, *Handbook of Economic Statistics, 1975,* Washington, D.C., August 1975.

Indonesian trade with the People's Republic of China takes place through Singapore and Hong Kong, but the total amount is insignificant in comparison with the volume of trade with the industrial democracies.

The case of Indonesia is particularly interesting not only because that country has 42 percent of the total Southeast Asian population, but also because it is a nonaligned but Western-oriented country (unlike Burma, which follows a policy of rigid isolation, anxiously avoiding contacts with the outside world). The other countries of Southeast Asia have at present or had until recently strong ties with outside powers: Malaysia and Singapore are still linked through the Five Power Treaty to Great Britain, Australia, and New Zealand; the Philippines and Thailand have military treaty relationships with the United States; Vietnam, Laos, and Cambodia have secret arrangements with the Soviet Union, with the People's Republic of China, and with one another.

Although all five members of the Association of Southeast Asian Nations (ASEAN) have diplomatic relations with the Soviet Union and three of them, Thailand, Malaysia, and the Philippines, also have diplomatic relations with the People's Republic of China, they have until now received economic and military assistance primarily from the countries toward which they have been leaning politically. The noncommunist states still rely on the industrial democracies for technology and higher education, while the communist states of Southeast Asia depend primarily on Soviet, Chinese, and Eastern European sources, although they would also like greater access on their own terms to technology and capital from the industrial democracies.

The total pattern of relationships with external powers has undergone major changes in the two decades since the July 1954 Geneva Conference and the April 1955 Bandung Conference, when the new states of Southeast Asia first asserted themselves as independent actors in world affairs. At that time, Thailand, the Philippines, and South Vietnam were firmly aligned with the West, dependent for their security on the United States. The territories which later became the Federation of Malaysia, and Singapore, were also firmly in the Western camp through the link of the British Commonwealth. North Vietnam, at that time the only communist country in the region, was trying to maintain its distance from the People's Republic of China—although it accepted Chinese military aid while being neglected by the Soviet Union. Burma, Indonesia, Laos, and Cambodia professed nonalignment in the cold war, although they maintained close economic and cultural links with their respective former colonial overlords and were ideologically closer to the West than to the communist world. Since the end of the war in Indochina, a significant shift toward real nonalignment is occurring among the formerly pro-Western countries, while the whole Indochinese peninsula is now controlled by local communist regimes. This substantially modified international environment provides an expanded arena for Sino-Soviet rivalry, the outcome of which is not predictable. Certainly, Western power in Southeast Asia has greatly declined as the result of military retrenchments and reduced security commitments, although Western economic and cultural influence remains strong.

In contrast with the 1950s, Great Britain has withdrawn its influential military presence from the region. American dominance came to an end following the Communist victories in Indochina in April 1975, although United States military forces are still present in the Philippines. However, the terms on which the bases are used are being renegotiated, and by the end of the next decade there might be no bases available to the United States in Southeast Asia. The residual United States military presence left in Thailand after the cessation of combat operations in Indochina was completely phased out in 1976, and only minor facilities are still available in that country. The era of Anglo-American hegemony, which resulted from Japan's defeat in 1945, is over.

The Soviets and the Chinese, despite heavy investments in the wars of Indochina, have made only modest advances to establish their presence in the region in ways that would give them military advantages in the Asian power balance. At the present time, Southeast Asia experiences less direct military pressure from external powers than perhaps at any time since the conquest of Malacca by the Portuguese in 1511, which initiated the age of colonialism. This is a partial fulfillment of what the nationalist elites, the potent antibodies created by the trauma of foreign invasion, had always wanted, and although the region is still highly vulnerable to the vagaries of the international market and to political manipulations by the great powers over which they have little influence, this is a step forward in the lengthy campaign for the elimination of the imperialist legacy.

Concomitantly with the waning of Western dominance, political institutions derived from American, British, Dutch, or French variants of representative government have been abandoned in Southeast Asia by the nationalist elites who had adopted them with considerable eagerness in the initial period of transition from colonialism to independent national existence. The oversimplified conclusion that well-working institutions were swept away by the withdrawing Western tide should be avoided. The constitutional arrangements adopted in the Philippines, Malaysia, Burma, Indonesia, and the noncommunist parts of Indochina at the time of independence were discarded because in indigenous settings they did not work, not because they became ideologically unfashionable, after the power balance shifted against the West. It is unlikely that the survival value of these alien political institutions would have been greater if politico-military Western influences in the region had remained stronger. The much longer historical experience of Latin America suggests a weak correlation between hegemonial control by the Western democracies and the lasting implantation of constitutional and representative government. Noncommunist Southeast Asia may be heading for the same nefarious treadmill from which Latin America has been unable to escape after a century and a half of political independence within a Western sphere of influence, namely alternation of civilian and military authoritarian regimes.

To appraise developments in the Indochinese peninsula after the great convulsions of 1975 seems premature. But in their first two years, the new communist regimes have shown little inclination to imitate closely the major communist powers or to become their satellites. While gratefully acknowledging the aid received from the Soviet Union during the war, the Lao Dong party of Vietnam continues to assert the spirit of independence which has characterized it for the last 30 years. Cambodia seems closer to Peking than to Moscow, but the macabre social engineering of the

Khmer Rouge has no close analogies in the recent history of the communist world and seems to be an indigenous innovation; and the seemingly amiable communization under way in Laos seems equally home-grown, not the result of the close ties the Pathet Lao have always had with the Lao Dong party of Vietnam.

During the first decades of their independent existence, the countries of Southeast Asia had been buffeted by forces beyond their control emanating from the major powers: pressure to join alliances, overt and covert interference in their internal affairs, economic dependence on a world market and on aid programs with a variety of strings attached, and intensive cultural penetration. Now the countries of Southeast Asia seem to be turning away from primary dependence on the major powers, looking inward, seeking practical formulas for self-reliance. The Southeast Asian states also seem to recognize the imperative of closing ranks with the other Third World nations and strengthening their solidarity in the sharpening North-South confrontation.

The Third World aim to reduce dependence on major powers seems to be requited by the flagging interest of the latter, who appear more concerned with one another than with the smaller nations from among which they previously recruited their clients. In the context of the balance-of-power politics being played in Southeast Asia, the countries of the region are of relatively minor importance. Not only do these countries offer little of current interest to the major powers, but they lack the resources without which it is difficult for them to influence the rest of the world. Even Vietnam, which has the largest and most effective military establishment in the region, is logistically too dependent on external sources of support to have a significant impact on extra-Asian relations, although, as will be argued later, it could become a formidable factor within Southeast Asia if it decided to seek a hegemonial role.

Mutual disengagement seems to be the dominant feature shaping relations between the countries of Southeast Asia and the major powers within and outside Asia at this time. The West is reducing its political and military involvement while maintaining economic ties both for their intrinsic commercial value and as an alternative mode of retaining influence. Japan is mostly interested in trade and views economic aid primarily as a means of retaining access to markets and to natural resources. The communist countries would like to expand their political influence and military presence but have not been willing or able to devote substantial economic resources to the achievement of these objectives. The changing role of the United States and the other major powers remains, in this context, a source of critical uncertainty for the policy makers of Southeast Asia. Although American influence is declining, Southeast Asian governments do not ignore the American factor when making policy decisions. It is still widely assumed in the region that the United States would intervene if the global balance or the intra-Asian equilibrium of forces were in jeopardy. But Southeast Asian governments do not expect the United States to intervene to counteract local insurgencies or interventions from within the region threatening the indigenous political regimes or their territorial integrity. They now hold somewhat disenchanted but realistic views concerning the credibility of the United States as a guarantor of the Asian status quo; they assume that American intervention is most likely to occur in the least likely contingencies, such as large-scale conflict among major powers, and is least likely to materialize in the most likely contingencies, such as insurgencies or local armed conflict between neighboring countries. In other words, the United States is still seen as a formidable global power, but is no longer considered the custodian of a particular regional order in Southeast Asia following the failure of its containment policy in Indochina.

The ruling elites of the region have not yet fully adjusted to these changed circumstances. They do not seem to realize that they can no longer count on the United States as an external guarantor of the prevailing social order. By abandoning its hegemonial role, the United States has opened Southeast Asia not only to the competition of all powers with interests and ambitions in the region but also to the competition of all social systems. This introduces new elements of uncertainty into the environment in which the governments of Southeast Asia will have to define their own future policies.

Currently, none of the four major powers is giving clear signals concerning its interests and intentions with regard to Southeast

Asia. The results of the November 1976 election in the United States gave no reliable indications as to whether the American people are turning inward or not. The Soviet Union seems to follow an opportunistic policy and no clear conclusion can be derived concerning the role it intends to play in Southeast Asia in the future, despite its substantial economic aid to Vietnam and Laos. In China, an era has come to an end with the death of Mao Tse-tung and Chou En-lai. The foreign policy of the moderates, who seem to be ahead in the succession struggle, is still unpredictable. In Japan, the scandal caused by the disclosure of the Lockheed bribes has accelerated the erosion of the political strength of the dominant Liberal-Democratic party, and the December 1976 elections have produced a new government of unknown durability. The uncertainties for Southeast Asia resulting from possible shifts in the policies of the major powers are, of course, compounded by the impact of these changes on the international system as a whole. Whether détente will last or not, how the Sino-Soviet conflict will evolve now that Mao is gone, and what foreign policy a different governmental coalition might set for Japan are among the more obvious questions. Consequently, the governments of Southeast Asia are faced with the task of adjusting their foreign policies to the likelihood of kaliedoscopic changes in the pattern of international relations.

Looking 10 years ahead to the mid-1980s, the safest forecast is probably that no major power will be permitted by the others to establish itself in a dominant role in Southeast Asia. In addition, the natural inclination of the Southeast Asian governments will be to seek to balance the presence of one country with that of another. For instance, if Japan's role expands and the United States seems unwilling to resume a leading role, the Soviet Union may be given opportunities which it would not otherwise receive, or Western Europe might receive preferential economic treatment, or the region might even become more receptive to Chinese influences. In any case, it is unlikely that a major power will again be able to turn Southeast Asia into its exclusive sphere of influence.

In the shorter run, political uncertainties will be compounded by the fact that the major powers are afflicted in varying degrees by economic difficulties. It is not yet evident that the United

States has won the battle against inflation and unemployment. Although the inherent strength of the American economy has been demonstrated in a number of ways during the last year and a recovery is now occurring, the public mood in the United States is very different from that in the 1960s which permitted the commitment of vast resources to the implementation of American foreign policy goals. President Carter has given no indication that he intends to pursue a dynamic foreign policy in Southeast Asia, while the Congress is limiting economic and military assistance, and private foreign investments are sluggish.

Japan is still seriously suffering from inflation and from the impact of global recession. The position of the yen has weakened and gloomy forecasters envisage the possibility of long-term economic stagnation following years of spectacular economic growth and expansion. Although Japan is likely to remain Southeast Asia's most important economic partner for the foreseeable future, economic stagnation could under certain circumstances produce relative scarcity of Japanese investment capital and have a retarding effect on the economic growth of Southeast Asia. Japan may also seek to limit its future investments in the region to avoid assuming the role of a hegemonial power.

The Soviet Union, although it acts like an ambitious and assertive global power, gives no evidence of planning significantly to expand its role in Southeast Asia, with the possible exception of its investment in Vietnam, which may be receiving 1 billion rubles in economic assistance this year. The absence of major Soviet aid programs in the noncommunist states of Southeast Asia is understandable. However tempting it may be to fill the void left by the United States, the Soviet Union has to cope with its own agricultural problems, intensify capital formation, respond to increasing domestic demand for consumer goods, keep up the strategic competition with the United States in the nuclear field, maintain or regain a position in the Middle East jeopardized by American diplomacy, and sustain a growing involvement in African affairs. Although Soviet trade with Southeast Asia is slowly expanding, unless the Soviet Union is prepared to play a major economic role, its influence will not grow decisively in those credit-hungry and growth-anxious countries.

The People's Republic of China, unlike the United States, Japan, and to a lesser but still significant degree the Soviet Union, has not been and will not be for some time a significant source of technology transfer, investment capital, or commercial credits to Southeast Asia. Its present influence in the area results primarily from the eagerness of vulnerable Southeast Asian governments to appease the Peking government, which they see as a potential source of support to local insurgents. Indonesia and Singapore may establish diplomatic relations with the People's Republic of China before too long, but contacts will remain limited and closely scrutinized.

Southeast Asian trade with the People's Republic of China, as with the Soviet Union, has been insignificant compared with trade with the United States, Japan, and Western Europe. Now that China is emerging as a potential exporter of oil, it may in a few years become a partial source of supply to some countries of Southeast Asia, such as Thailand and the Philippines, and to some extent a competitor of Indonesia, especially in the Japanese market. Whether China's growing oil production and its increasing capacity to export grains will become sources of enhanced leverage in Southeast Asia will depend on Peking's willingness to grant commercial credits rather than to demand cash payments in foreign exchange, which are much needed for China's own development-related imports.

On balance, none of the major powers seems eager at this time—each for its own particular reasons—to increase substantially its political and economic investments in Southeast Asia, with the noted exception of Soviet aid to Vietnam, which is given for strategic purposes. All major powers, without exception, have been affected during the last two decades by the volatility of Southeast Asian politics. No state in the region has proved in the long run to be either a reliable political ally or a reliable economic partner and no commitments have been immune to sudden reversals. Consequently, the states of Southeast Asia may find their opportunities to play off one major power against another drastically curtailed, with a corresponding loss of diplomatic flexibility and reduced prospects for external assistance on concessional terms.

The four major powers are not the only ones that have an impact on the affairs of Southeast Asia. If it succeeds in harnessing its economic resources, India might give, in the next decade, freer rein to its latent hegemonial aspirations in the Indian Ocean. The Southeast Asian governments may face new complications in determining their foreign policy course in the 1980s if India, which has historically inspired concern in its eastern neighbors, becomes more assertive. In the very recent past, Southeast Asia had less cause to be apprehensive of India because of India's obsession with Pakistan, its concern with China, and the moral inhibitions of the Gandhi-Nehru tradition which were still operating. But India is a potential major power and the Southeast Asians may discover either the usefulness of closer ties with that giant state or the necessity to develop countervailing influences to an increased Indian presence in the region.

There are indications that the oil-rich Arab countries of the Middle East are perceiving the political opportunities created by their vast financial resources. As of mid-1976, Indonesia, and perhaps other countries in Southeast Asia, began to view financial assistance from the Middle East as an important addition to traditional sources of capital from the Western international consortium and possibly, in the future, as a politically acceptable alternative to past dependence on the major industrial democracies.

Also potentially significant are smaller and more remote countries such as Iran and Australia, because of their active foreign policies, economic and military potential, intense interest in the situation in the Indian Ocean, and inherently unpredictable orientation 10 to 15 years hence.

Under its present ruler, Iran is planning to become a significant military factor in the Indian Ocean. It will probably have the means to pursue such a policy for at least the lifespan of one generation. But its foreign policy is not firmly anchored in the country's political tradition. The whim of the Shah or the hazards of succession could conceivably alter the situation, despite Iran's logistical dependence on the United States, at least through the 1980s.

For Southeast Asia the future role of these medium powers is not a negligible consideration. If India, Iran, Saudi Arabia, and Australia were to play economic, political, and military balancing roles in Southeast Asia, their presence would reduce the impact of the policies of the great powers on the region and help protect it against great-power hegemony. Active cooperation with any or all of these medium powers is likely to be eagerly sought by Southeast Asian governments seeking to prevent unwanted great power influence. The diffusion of political, economic, and military power could create in the 1980s new alignments which can not be anticipated simply by extrapolating from the present situation.

FOUR

Hegemonial Aspirants in Southeast Asia

Current discussions about the future world order have popularized the concept of regional powers which, although they are not capable of playing a major role on a global scale, are expected to assume a dominant position in their respective part of the world by virtue of their human and natural resources and of the self-confidence and sense of destiny engendered by their abundant material endowment. Brazil, India, Indonesia, Iran, and Nigeria are usually named as candidates for regional power status in the 1980s. This vision of a tiered global power structure would place such medium powers hierarchically just below the five entities which are the power centers of the multipolar world of the 1970s (the United States, the Soviet Union, the People's Republic of China, the European Community, and Japan), having in turn replaced the bipolar world of the 1960s.

The regional hegemony theorists expect medium powers to create around themselves a regional order or limited sphere of influence, possibly as the result of a tacit devolution of responsibilities by global powers interested in lightening their burdens or anxious to avoid confrontations resulting from rivalry with other global powers, but unwilling to yield the field to their principal competitors. The idea is not without merit, as a global power is more likely to be willing to concede a dominant regional role to a medium power which cannot challenge its global prominence than to another global power whose incremental gains might threaten to upset the global balance.

Interest in the potential role of medium powers in regional affairs may be a reflection of the growing desire in American policy-making circles to retrench from the responsibilities of a "policeman of the world" role without creating opportunities for Soviet gains in international influence and power. An enhanced role for countries like Brazil, India, Indonesia, Iran, and Nigeria, which are expected to be friendly to the United States, seems a promising alternative in areas from which the United States wishes to withdraw or into which it does not want to enter as a guarantor of the regional order. Although these vague concepts have never received official sanction from those responsible for the conduct of American foreign relations and have not yet been clarified by governmental or academic analysts, they have become a recurrent theme in speculations about the future shape of a world order.

INDONESIA: POTENTIAL AND ASPIRATIONS FOR REGIONAL HEGEMONY

It is abstractly conceivable that if all the major powers abstain from exerting controlling influence in a region by use of their superior military, political, economic, and other resources, the most powerful country within that region could establish itself in a hegemonial position. In the case of Southeast Asia, such preconditions are indeed emerging, as suggested above. These are conditions in which Indonesia could assert, in principle, a leadership role in view of its privileged location, large population, and apparent abundance of natural resources. A glance at Table 1 shows that the population of Indonesia exceeds in numbers the combined population of the next three largest countries in the region, the Philippines, Vietnam, and Thailand. Table 2 shows that it has also the largest total GNP and volume of foreign trade in Southeast Asia. On the other hand, it has one of the lowest levels of per capita income, exceeding only Burma and Indochina, and is still in an early stage of economic development, having lost precious time in the first 20 years after its proclamation of independence, first because of the anticolonial war it had to fight against the Netherlands and then because of the mismanagement of its resources by the romantic-nationalist government of the late President Sukarno.

Since 1966, the "New Order" of President Suharto has made serious efforts to stabilize the economy, previously plagued by hyperinflation, and to create the preconditions for economic takeoff by achieving self-sufficiency in food and by rehabilitating the economic infrastructure which had been run down constantly since the end of the Dutch colonial administration in March 1942. But despite some real progress, notably in the production of rice and in the growth of extractive industries, there has also been massive backsliding. The national oil company, Pertamina, ran into very serious financial difficulties in the spring of 1975, weakening temporarily Indonesia's foreign exchange position. But two years later, in June 1977, foreign exchange reserves amounted to $2 billion and the general elections of May 1977 indicated continued confidence in the Suharto government, which is likely to be able to maintain its current steady course for another five years.

But Indonesia cannot count indefinitely on natural resources as an alternative to sustained and disciplined development efforts. For a country with its population and anticipated energy consumption, Indonesia has modest proven oil reserves. The most optimistic estimate, for January 1, 1976, mentioned 14 billion barrels—then 2.1 percent of the total global proven oil reserves.[11] Some pessimistic recent estimates accept only half of that figure. But taking the highest figure and applying current sales prices, without discounting interest for sales that will occur many years hence, the total value of Indonesia's currently most important natural resource would not exceed about $175 billion. Using 1975 population figures, this amounts to less than $1,300 per capita and, if the 1990 population projection from Table 2 is used, less than $900 per capita. This is not sufficient capital to create new jobs for all claimants in the 1980s in one of the world's poorer countries. But Indonesia also has other natural resources, not all of which are depleting, including fertile though overcrowded soil and an excellent climate for tropical agriculture,

[11]Sevinc Carlson, *Indonesia's Oil,* Georgetown University Center for Strategic and International Studies, 1976, p. 21.

substantial though qualitatively uneven forest resources, and promising though not exceptional amounts of metallic ores, coal, and natural gas.

The overall level of general and technical education is still low, with 72 percent literacy in the 6 to 16 years age group, and a limited reservoir of managerial and administrative skills. The constraints on rapid economic growth are obvious; it does not therefore seem likely that Indonesia will become a major economic power in the coming decade.

Far from seeking a hegemonial economic role in Southeast Asia, the Indonesian government is trying to protect its infant industries without inflicting excessive costs on a population whose purchasing power is among the lowest in the world. In fact, Indonesia's efforts to protect its own economy have led to complaints by other Southeast Asian governments that Indonesia is parochial and uncooperative on issues of regional economic growth. After the first summit meeting in February 1976 in Bali of the heads of government of ASEAN, the story circulated that there had been strong disappointment about Indonesia's opposition even to future trade liberalization within ASEAN. The chief architect of Indonesia's economic policy since 1966, Professor Widjojo Nitisastro, Coordinating Minister for Economic Affairs and chairman of the National Planning Agency, offered his version of the events during a lengthy conversation we had in Jakarta on June 23, 1976.

According to Professor Widjojo, ASEAN had not achieved much in its first eight years because the economic agencies of the member countries were only sporadically involved in ASEAN affairs. Understandings reached on economic issues were primarily politically motivated and were not very workable. When the decision was reached to hold an ASEAN summit meeting, President Suharto became interested in promoting his concept of regional resilience through ASEAN economic cooperation. An earlier meeting of economic and planning ministers in November 1975 undertook the task of developing a program based on classical economics as expounded by professors G. Haberler and C. Kindleberger. Proposals for an ASEAN common market and customs union were put forward. In principle, Professor Widjojo remarked, the introduction of free trade seems easy: duties are first frozen, then reduced, then abolished. The end result is a larger market and incentives to greater production. But Indonesian advisers feared that a free-trade situation would create equity problems where the participating economies lacked common starting points. The economic growth achieved by free trade would have favored the already economically strong members and increased political tensions in the region.

Professor Widjojo believes that if ASEAN is to have a permanent economic function, areas of potential tension such as maldistribution of gains among unequal partners in a customs union arrangement must be identified in advance; otherwise the cause to be promoted will be harmed rather than helped. Indonesia has suggested, therefore, that instead of establishing a free-trade area, ASEAN member states devise creative mechanisms of economic cooperation which suit common needs without raising the problems caused by free trade. Thus, Indonesia proposed preferential trading agreements which would give ASEAN members priority in the supply and purchase of food and energy, especially when there is a shortage. This would test the willingness of the ASEAN countries to cooperate with each other.

Besides cooperation in food and energy, Indonesia proposed that ASEAN countries favor imports from each other through administrative measures rather than through tariffs. For example, it should be possible for Indonesia's government agencies to buy cement or superphosphates from the Philippines rather than from Japan. Indonesia also proposed that there be more credits granted within the ASEAN group of states.

Although other ASEAN participants accepted Indonesia's proposals in November 1975, the states more in favor of free trade later claimed that Indonesia was in fact undermining ASEAN unity by rejecting bold and concrete economic proposals which would advance ASEAN. ASEAN participants from Singapore and the Philippines were the most dissatisfied: the Philippines is generally pro–free trade in the classic tradition and Singapore had been using free trade as a lure to potential European investors in its industries.

Indonesia's interest in ASEAN economic cooperation was demonstrated after the Bali summit meeting when the economic ministers of the five countries met again in Kuala Lumpur and agreed on the establishment of five ASEAN industrial projects, such as a urea fertilizer plant in Indonesia, intended to meet the requirements of the whole region. All five projects will be joint ASEAN ventures, with the host country holding a majority of shares, and the respective products will receive preferential treatment through special trading arrangements.

ASEAN has also agreed on consultations preceding the establishment of purely national projects, such as petrochemical plants or steel mills, to avoid unnecessary duplication of productive capacity in the five countries. Other projects will be set up aiming at complementarity, for instance in the automotive industry. In this context, Professor Widjojo remarked that ways to promote economic cooperation between developing countries still require thinking and experimentation. ASEAN can perform a useful function in this field, as well as finding ways to protect its member countries from world food and energy crises and by developing common positions on world economic issues, including the pressing matter of commodity prices. Specific agreements to implement these decisions were made in February 1977.

Indonesia's cautious regional economic policy reinforces President Suharto's determination to avoid fear or resentment among Indonesia's smaller neighbors, especially those countries where ethnic, linguistic, or religious factors in common with Indonesia could be exploited for expansionist purposes by an Indonesian government with imperialist ambitions.

The national languages of Indonesia and Malaysia are identical and have been further unified by the recent adoption of common spelling rules. Ethnically, there are many ties between the Malay population on the peninsula and various Indonesian tribal groups, especially in Sumatra. On the island of Borneo, divided between Indonesia and Malaysia as the respective heirs of Dutch and British colonialism, the native lands of indigenous tribes do not always coincide with international borders arbitrarily traced through virgin forests. The Muslim population in Mindanao and the Sulu Archipelago has more in common with the indigenous population of Malaysian Sabah and Indonesian Kalimantan than with the Christian Filipinos to the north, who have been and still are traditional enemies. But whereas the Philippines and Malaysia have been engaged for more than a decade in a subdued but bitter territorial controversy, Indonesia has carefully avoided any involvement which might appear self-serving. At no time during the decade since the Suharto regime came to power has it betrayed either directly or indirectly the desire to assume politically or militarily a hegemonial position in the region, nor have its actions betrayed any hidden intentions to embark on the road to glory and aggrandizement. On the contrary, President Suharto and his aides have played down the fact that Indonesia is the world's fifth most populous country or that it could become the leader of a pan-Malay movement.

This policy has been motivated in part by the desire to erase the very unfavorable memories left in Southeast Asia by President Sukarno's "confrontation" with Malaysia and by the grandiloquent style of his foreign policy, but also by the recognition that in view of Indonesia's massive domestic problems the danger of diverting resources toward a regional policy of "manifest destiny" must be resisted because it would involve military expenditures which Indonesia could not afford.

This policy is unlikely to change, unless major social convulsions induced by population pressure, mismanagement, or historical accident give a demagogic agitator control of the Indonesian government. Under normal circumstances, national resources will be devoted to economic development by any Indonesian government in the next decade. The present regime or a likeminded successor is not likely to resort to external adventures as an escape from internal difficulties. Even under favorable assumptions Indonesia will still be a poor country by 1985. The Indonesian Minister for Research, Professor Sumitro Djojohadikusumo, reported to a cabinet session in early June 1976 that "if the development process continues to run smoothly the per capita income will be raised from $109 in 1975 to $245 in 1985."[12] The estimate was based on an average rate of growth of 8.1 percent during the 1975–1980 period and 8.87 percent during the 1980–

[12]Which figures to use with regard to the Indonesian per capita GNP is a tantalizing but probably unsolvable problem. In his *Address of State* delivered in Jakarta on August 16, 1976, on the eve of Indonesia's thirty-first Independence Day, President Suharto stated explicitly that per capita GNP had increased from $89 in 1965 to $143 in 1975.

1985 period. Such high growth rates cannot be achieved without very careful management of resources, leaving no surplus for external adventures. Professor Sumitro estimated that the population of Indonesia would increase from 132 million in 1975 to 167 million in 1985, of which 103 million would be concentrated at that time in Java and Madura, bringing the population density there to 767 persons per square kilometer and increasing the labor force by 800,000 a year in those two already overcrowded islands. The conclusion presented to the cabinet was that in view of these population trends, the government's development policy should be geared mainly to supplying basic needs such as food, clothing, housing, health services, education, and employment opportunities.[13]

The recent incorporation of the former Portuguese colony of East Timor does not contradict this interpretation of Indonesia's current lack of interest in political hegemony or territorial expansion. The chain of events which resulted on June 29, 1976, in the Indonesian government's decision to approve the integration of East Timor as the twenty-seventh province of Indonesia started with the announcement by President Spinola of Portugal on May 16, 1974, that democratic freedom would be given to the people in Portuguese overseas territories.

After the change of regime in Portugal, political parties emerged in East Timor. Factional struggle degenerated into civil war during 1975. About 40,000 refugees escaped to the Indonesian part of the island, while increasingly violent armed clashes occurred between activist groups which favored either independence or federation with Portugal or accession to Indonesia. Yet only after a leftist group known as Fretilin proclaimed the "People's Democratic Republic of East Timor" on November 28, 1975, did Indonesia intervene militarily on December 7 and capture Dili, the capital of the territory, chasing the Fretilin forces into the back country, from whence sporadic armed resistance continues. Covert operations assisted pro-Indonesians in Timor's People's Assembly who chose integration with Indonesia. But these manipulations were not a portent of things to come elsewhere in the region.

[13]*The New Standard,* Jakarta, July 3, 1976.

Because Indonesian military intervention in East Timor was a direct response to the imminent threat of having a leftist regime established as an enclave within the perimeter of the Indonesian archipelago, it has not been viewed by the other ASEAN countries as a manifestation of Indonesian expansionism, but rather as a way of forestalling an irreversible political development that could have given the Soviet Union or the People's Republic of China a foothold in the region as patrons of an economically unviable ministate. As could be expected, the Communist powers denounced the Indonesian intervention, but they did nothing to prevent the destruction of the leftist Fretilin movement. The military operations in East Timor may have unintentionally reassured Indonesia's neighbors. Although the campaign received sparse coverage by the media, it became well known in capitals of the neighboring countries that the Indonesian armed forces encountered more serious difficulties in dealing with a few thousand hastily armed Fretilin combatants than had been anticipated.

For more than a decade the Indonesian armed forces had abstained from spending sparse public funds for the acquisition of modern equipment and for sustained training. As a result, the combat readiness of the troops employed in East Timor was low, thus showing that Indonesia's military capabilities are not suitable for an expansionist role in Southeast Asia or even for that of senior partner in an alliance for the common defense of the ASEAN countries.[14] Current plans envisage only a limited improvement in Indonesia's defensive capability. Indonesia's defense planners are deeply concerned by the Communist victories in Indochina, which gave the forces of the Socialist Republic of Vietnam large quantities of modern American weapons. The

[14]According to the International Institute of Strategic Studies, the Indonesian Army had in 1975 a strength of 200,000 of which about one-third were engaged in civil and administrative duties. The total level of forces of the Navy and the Air Force was 66,000, and their equipment consisted of a small number of obsolete items, including 3 submarines (Soviet W-class), 9 frigates, 10 amphibious vessels, 47 combat aircraft (2 B-26 Invader, 17 CA-27 Avon-Sabre, 11 F-51D Mustang, and 17 T-33A), and 65 transport aircraft (of which 8 are C-130Bs and 37 are C-47s). Source: The International Institute for Strategic Studies, *The Military Balance 1975–1976*, London, 1976, pp. 54–55.

reaction in Jakarta after May 1975 has been that under the changed circumstances created by the American defeat and withdrawal and the emergence of Vietnam as a major military factor in the region, Indonesia's defense plans would have to be reviewed and the readiness of its armed forces improved. But that revised threat assessment happened to coincide with a severe liquidity crisis which depleted the country's foreign exchange reserves.

Having lost, due to political circumstances, a total investment of about $1.2 billion in Soviet military equipment, for which the Soviet Union refused to provide maintenance and spare parts after 1967, the Indonesian armed forces are now acquiring a much more modest capability from the West. American assistance does not seek to redress the military balance in Southeast Asia, which has been so decisively upset by the Communist victories in Indochina. In the five years from FY 1973 through FY 1977 Indonesia received only $79.9 million in military assistance grants (MAP) (to be discontinued after FY 1978), $54.7 million in military assistance credits (FMS) (the figure for FY 1978 will not exceed $40 million), and $11.3 million in training grants—a total of $145.9 million. Obviously, American air and naval power, based with somewhat uncertain tenure in the Philippines, remains for the foreseeable future the only counterpoise to Vietnamese military domination of the region.

After decisively altering the strategic balance in the Pacific in 1966 by destroying the Communist party of Indonesia without any external support, and by terminating the special relationships with the Soviet Union and the People's Republic of China, Indonesian military leaders were expecting in the last decade to receive large-scale military assistance from the United States. When the $1.5 billion Five-Year Modernization Plan for the Armed Forces of the Republic of Korea was approved by the United States government in 1970, the Indonesian military leaders felt that they should receive military assistance on the same scale. Later, they hoped to receive American surplus weapons as the United States forces were withdrawing from South Vietnam. The need for large-scale American military assistance was felt even more strongly in Jakarta after the collapse of South Vietnam in April 1975. Disappointed by the lack of American support,

Indonesian military leaders are currently living with the unre-solved dilemma of accepting either lack of defense readiness for the foreseeable future or a serious curtailment of economic growth if resources are transferred to weapons acquisition programs.

Except for token American military assistance, there are at present no acceptable sources of outside support for an Indone-sian military build-up. Even if the Soviet Union were prepared to fill the vacuum, the present Indonesian military leadership is determined not to renew logistical dependency on the state that supplied it substantial amounts of sophisticated weapons in the early 1960s and then rendered the whole modern inventory of the Indonesian armed forces useless by refusing for political reasons to provide maintenance and spare parts. Furthermore, the likelihood of another massive Soviet military assistance pro-gram to Indonesia is very low both because the present Indone-sian leadership would certainly refuse the Soviets any military facilities as a quid pro quo and because the principal rationale for such a program—namely to create a balance of power against Vietnam—would conflict with the obvious Soviet interest to maintain close relations with the government in Hanoi.

Consistent with its modest military capabilities, Indonesia has expressed no interest in transforming ASEAN into a military alliance or in asserting a leadership role in regional defense. The "Declaration of ASEAN Concord" signed in Bali on Feburary 24, 1976, provided for "continuation of cooperation on a non-ASEAN basis between the member states in security matters in accordance with their mutual needs and interests." The non-aligned tradition has very strong roots in Indonesian public opinion and a military alliance is considered incompatible with a "free and active foreign policy." An alliance would link Indo-nesia with countries that have military ties with the United States or with the British Commonwealth and would make it more dif-ficult to claim that Indonesia has no ties with either of the great powers. Indonesia fears that military ties of a multilateral nature would cause resentment and apprehension within Southeast Asia that it was trying to dominate its neighbors. This position could, of course, change if Vietnam became a clear and present danger to ASEAN and if the other governments urged Indonesia to join them in preparing for their common defense.

The conclusion seems warranted that, despite its size and a certain sense of "manifest destiny," Indonesia is not likely to assert hegemonial claims in Southeast Asia as long as the views of the Suharto regime remain national policy and present conditions prevail. It is not inconceivable, nevertheless, that a new leadership, with a less rational set of national priorities, could revive Sukarno's romantic aspirations of past years. A radical-nationalist regime could decide to divert a substantial part of the proceeds of Indonesia's exports from developmental capital investments to the modernization of the armed forces, with the intent of projecting Indonesian power throughout Southeast Asia. Substantial resources could be mobilized over the next 10 years for military expenditures if economic development were to be sacrificed. The International Bank for Reconstruction and Development has estimated that Indonesia's projected exports could increase from $5,180 million in 1975 to $11,350 million in 1980 and to $22,000 million in 1985 at current prices. If a regime bent on adventure could at the same time manage the export sector of the economy well enough to turn these export projections into reality, and if the world market for its products was favorable, Indonesia could emerge in the future as a military factor of regional significance, albeit at the cost of the hopes for relief from abject poverty of its rapidly growing population.

In view of the present condition of the Indonesian armed forces, which are a mixture of old soldiers overdue for retirement and young soldiers poorly trained and without combat experience, and considering the lead times involved in the procurement of sophisticated weapons and the training required to operate and maintain them, it might take a decade or more after the basic decision to modernize the armed forces had been made before Indonesia would have the military attributes of a regional power. In fact, while it is easy to imagine the political circumstances that would turn Indonesia toward a "guns rather than butter" policy of regional adventure, it is difficult to visualize the modality for the rapid development of organizational skills and unity of purpose required for the effective implementation of such a policy.

VIETNAM: POTENTIAL AND ASPIRATIONS FOR REGIONAL HEGEMONY

Vietnam is the only other nation-state in Southeast Asia which would, during the next decade or so, have a sufficient military and financial edge on its neighbors to assume a hegemonial role in the region. It has been demonstrated that while Indonesia might have such a capability, it is not likely to have the requisite will to direct Indonesian resources to that end. Vietnam, on the other hand, might have the will. In fact, Indonesian rearmament would likely only occur as a reaction to Vietnamese hegemonial claims, motivated perhaps by a deliberate Vietnamese policy to scare the governments of Southeast Asia into the diversion of financial resources from economic development to military preparedness, in the hope that the retardation of economic growth would accelerate the radicalization of the population and enhance the chances of Communist parties.

Such a specter has been raised. Within four days after the conclusion of the ASEAN summit meeting, on February 28, 1976, an authoritative editorial in *Nhan Dan,* rebroadcast by Radio Hanoi, created considerable apprehension in Southeast Asian capitals. As monitored by the Foreign Broadcast Information Service, the article, entitled "Unprecedented Opportunity for Southeast Asian Nations," proclaimed that "the victories of the Vietnamese, Cambodian, and Lao peoples have had the effect of setting forth the Southeast Asian peoples' struggle for independence and freedom as an example and strongly stimulated this struggle." The statement which was considered particularly ominous proclaimed:

The Vietnamese people fully support the struggle of the peoples of the Southeast Asian nations for independence, democracy, peace and social progress. Our people's struggle against U.S. imperialist aggression, for independence and freedom, which involves many sacrifices, is aimed also at supporting the just struggle of the neighboring nations and contributing to building a Southeast Asia of peace and friendly cooperation.

This promise of support was followed by an exhortation for the overthrow of the existing governments:

The struggle of the Southeast Asian peoples is enjoying favorable conditions and has the brightest prospects ever seen in their history of the past century. By intensifying this struggle, the peoples of the Southeast Asian countries will certainly foil all neocolonialist schemes and tricks of the U.S. imperialists and reactionaries, restore true national independence and sovereignty and restore the ownership of the Southeast Asian region to the Southeast Asians. This is a trend compatible with the law of historic evolution and cannot be reversed by any reactionary force.[15]

Coming from the victorious Lao Dong leaders of Vietnam, re-positories of unparalleled revolutionary experience and posses-sors of vast stores of captured American weapons, it was not a message to be overlooked either by the governments or by the undergrounds of Southeast Asia. Of course, not all inflammatory statements are followed by action, but because the dedication of the Vietnamese leaders to the cause of revolution is not open to doubt and their past record shows that they study their moves carefully and are not prone to emotional and impulsive gestures, the statement elicited considerable concern in the ASEAN countries.

In July senior Vietnamese diplomats visited ASEAN capitals, stating publicly that their country intended to export rice, timber, and coal, not revolution, and that the American weapons captured in 1975 were no threat to their ASEAN neighbors, as they were to be used only for internal security and for the defense of Vietnamese sovereignty.[16]

The ASEAN governments, which have all had their share of bitter experiences with communism in their respective countries, remain skeptical. Uncertain about the intentions of the Lao Dong leadership, they assume that at some future time, perhaps after a period of Vietnamese reconstruction and development for which foreign assistance is currently sought, the Hanoi government could become as ruthless in seeking hegemony in Southeast Asia as it was in the past 30 years when it imposed gigantic sacrifices on its own people in its struggle against the West. It is not a far-

---

[15]Foreign Broadcast Information Service, *Daily Report Asia & Pacific,* Monday, 1 March 1976, pp. K4–6.

[16]Deputy Foreign Minister Phan Hien's statement to the press, reported in *The New Standard,* Jakarta, July 24, 1976.

fetched assumption that if the leaders of the Lao Dong party have or develop such regional ambitions, Vietnam could become a twentieth-century Prussia in Southeast Asia. The team which is carrying out Ho Chi Minh's testament is a unique group of men who have been able to avoid factional strife for more than 30 years, unlike any other Communist party. The Lao Dong's collective leadership was able to defeat first France and then the United States politically as well as militarily and managed to obtain assistance both from the Soviet Union and from the People's Republic of China, despite the rivalry between the two communist powers, without becoming the satellite of either.

It can safely be assumed, moreover, that the morale of the Vietnamese leadership, of its political cadres, and of the armed forces under its command, is and will remain extremely high. The inner strength, cohesion, and self-assurance of the Vietnamese leadership are demonstrated by the speed with which the unification of North and South has proceeded. It was completed within one year of the April 1975 victory, despite more than 20 years of separation and contrary to the predictions of foreign experts that rivalries between the leadership in the two segments of the country and the great disparity of their economic and social systems would delay reunification for at least five years. And unlike the Southeast Asian countries which do not have well-developed methods of mass mobilization and population control, Vietnam can continue to impose material deprivations on its people without having to resort to demagogic agitation or to show instant successes. This will allow it to pursue a calculating, carefully planned foreign policy, much more flexible and vigorous than that of its less regimented neighbors.

Added to these political advantages, Vietnam's military capabilities put it into a class by itself in its part of the world. Its actual military capability decisively exceeds even the potential collective strength of its noncommunist Southeast Asian neighbors. Even more significantly, the present forces of the Socialist Republic of Vietnam outnumber probably by a substantial margin those currently deployed by the People's Republic of China in its military regions close to Southeast Asia. According to the September 1976 estimates of the International Institute for Strategic Studies, the Socialist Republic of Vietnam has at present total armed forces of 615,000 organized in 18 infantry divisions, 2 training divisions, 1 artillery command of 10 regiments, 3 armored regiments, about 15 independent infantry regiments, 20 SAM regiments, 50 AA artillery regiments, plus 50,000 armed security forces and an armed militia of about 1,500,000. The military of the former Republic of Vietnam are not included in these figures. Although it is estimated that some 200,000 South Vietnamese, including many military, are in communist "reeducation" camps, one can assume that a substantial number of the 500,000 military of the regular Republic of Vietnam Armed Forces (RVNAF), many of whom received training by the United States in the use of sophisticated weapons, will be absorbed into the People's Army of Vietnam (PAVN) following screening and indoctrination. During 30 years of combat, the PAVN acquired unusual skills in logistic improvisation, giving it the capacity to make use of captured equipment even in very difficult circumstances. With American supply stores and American-trained personnel available, it is possible that PAVN will be able to use United States–produced equipment long after other defense establishments would have been forced to discard it for lack of spare parts and maintenance. On July 9, 1976, the Department of Defense released the following summary of American arms captured in Indochina:

TABLE 4
American Arms Captured in Indochina

	Vietnam	Cambodia
M-41A3	300	0
M-48A3	250	0
M-113 APCs	1,200	181
105mm howitzers	1,000	265
155mm howitzers	250	22
175mm self-propelled guns	80	0
M-16 rifles	791,000	155,000
Rifles (various other types)	857,580	104,000

TABLE 4 (Continued)
American Arms Captured in Indochina

	Vietnam	Cambodia
M-60 machine guns	15,000	320
M-79 grenade launchers	47,000	78,500
Light antitank weapons (LAW)	63,000	0
.45-cal pistols	90,000	24,000
60, 81, 90mm* mortars	12,000	3,100
PRC 10/25 radios	42,000	9,700
VRC-46 radios	6,000	0
F-5A/B aircraft	51	0
F-5E aircraft	22	0
A-37 aircraft	113	0
A-1 aircraft	36	0
C-130A aircraft	10	0
C-119 aircraft	40	0
C-7 aircraft	40	0
UH-1 helicopter	430	24
CH-47 helicopter	36	0
O-1/O-2	159	18
AC/EC/VC/RC-47 aircraft	36	7
T-28 aircraft	0	22
C-123 aircraft	0	7
T-41 aircraft	22	12
Ammunition†	130,000 tons	235,970 rounds
Trucks (¼, ¾, and 2½ ton)	42,000	4,600
Naval ships/craft	940	115

*There is no 90mm mortar in the United States inventory; however, some 200 recoilless rifles—90mm—of United States manufacture are estimated to have been captured by the Vietnamese Communists.

†The majority of ammunition captured is 40mm, 60mm, 81mm, and 105mm.

SOURCE: DIA/APPR 94-75 and 103-75, June 1975.

Since the cessation of hostilities in April 1975 there has been a slight reduction in the standing army, but there is still a minimum of two years of compulsory military service. Taking into account the number of combat-experienced veterans of both PAVN and RVNAF, the mobilization potential of the Socialist Republic of Vietnam is formidable. By contrast, the noncommunist countries of Southeast Asia are weak and ill-prepared both individually and collectively. These countries are not military allies and are not prepared to act as a single military entity. Table 5 enumerates the noncommunist forces in Southeast Asia as of September 1976.

TABLE 5
Noncommunist Military Forces

	Manpower	Tanks	Seagoing Ships	Combat Aircraft
Burma	169,500	0	47	10
Indonesia	246,000	125	108	30
Malaysia	62,300	0	44	50
Philippines	78,000	7	93	56
Singapore	31,000	75	18	97
Thailand	210,000	195	75	179
Totals	796,800	402	385	422

SOURCE: The International Institute for Strategic Studies, *The Military Balance 1976–1977*, London, 1977, pp. 54–61.

The International Institute for Strategic Studies estimated that North Vietnam had a GNP of $1.8 billion in 1972 and devoted $584 million to military expenditures in 1970. If Soviet and Chinese military assistance were included in the GNP, in wartime the government was able to mobilize over 32 percent of GNP for military expenditures. Assuming, now that hostilities have ceased and reconstruction is under way, that the per capita GNP averages no less than $100 for the whole country and is growing, at present the Socialist Republic of Vietnam would have a GNP of no less than $4.3 billion. If in the future it chooses to spend again at the wartime rate of 32 percent, it could devote $1.376 billion to military expenditures, given its present GNP, and more in the future when its GNP is bound to increase.

Will the Vietnamese economy be able to sustain on a long-term basis a high level of military preparedness? The question is difficult to answer, as it depends as much on political will as on economic means. After 30 years of turmoil the Vietnamese people certainly need a period of peace, reconstruction, and development with all the outside assistance they can get. The leaders are aging and have been under great stress for a long time. Whatever their secret hopes and aspirations may be for a dominant future position in Southeast Asia, these intentions are not going to be made public at this time, when they would deprive Vietnam of the goodwill of the international community and might even create antagonism between the Vietnamese people and its leaders. If the Lao Dong leaders have messianic aspirations in the region, their past record would suggest that the achievement of such goals would be planned with the same patient cunning that characterized the successful campaigns against France and the United States.

If Vietnam could count on the noninvolvement of the major powers, it could certainly take successful military action against any or all of its neighbors on the Southeast Asian mainland. Thailand and Malaysia, standing alone, would not be likely to offer lengthy resistance to Vietnamese attacks through Communist Laos and Cambodia. Singapore would be defenseless across the causeway from a Communist-controlled Malaysia and would have to seek an immediate accommodation. Indonesia and the Philippines are, of course, not directly vulnerable to Vietnam's land forces, being protected by the South China Sea. But their vulnerability to externally supported insurgencies would be greatly enhanced if their ASEAN partners were communized first.

If the Lao Dong leaders adopted such ambitious long-term plans, they could certainly afford to be even more patient than they proved to be for the achievement of their domestic goals and to wait before each move for favorable circumstances. With a

69

flexible timetable and stubborn determination, the next 15 years might well allow the implementation of an action program that would appear utopian to a less tough, self-confident, and successful group. An obvious scenario would be to create civil war conditions in Thailand and Malaysia, either simultaneously or in sequence, making the proclamation of countergovernments in "liberated" areas sufficiently plausible to facilitate their recognition by a number of politically like-minded governments. As both Thailand and Malaysia have relatively weak and vulnerable governments, sustained terrorist campaigns requiring only small numbers of activists might be sufficient to create the appropriate setting. Sustained by international propaganda and using techniques which have been continuously refined for over half a century, such countergovernments could then turn to the Vietnamese government and request its military support. Having forced the United States to withdraw from Indochina after eight years of large-scale combat, the Lao Dong leaders would not be unduly concerned by the prospect of American intervention on behalf of Thailand, which had demanded the withdrawal of all United States forces, or of Malaysia, which never had security arrangements with the United States. If international propriety were observed by disguising aggression as a response to the appeal of allegedly legitimate governments, Vietnam could move in with ease. The Angolan episode and possible similar events in the future would not be lost on the Lao Dong leaders.

In any case, any Southeast Asian regimes seeking change will find a model in the Socialist Republic of Vietnam. Made glamorous in the eyes of its neighbors by its military and political successes, Vietnam will proudly continue to experiment with its own patterns of social and economic development. If successful, its influence in the area will be considerably magnified. Students of history know that victorious countries become trend setters, often regardless of the intrinsic value of their example. France in the eighteenth century, Great Britain in the nineteenth century, and the United States in the twentieth century are outstanding, but by no means unique, examples.

What, then, will be the role of the Socialist Republic of Vietnam in Southeast Asia in the coming decades? It is not likely to concentrate exclusively on reconstruction and development for long. It will offer its revolutionary elan for emulation and will proselytize with increasing militancy in the gatherings of the Third World, to which it already has full access, and in the United Nations, of which it will undoubtedly become a member. It may become a more appealing model than China to radical elements in neighboring countries, for China defies imitation because of its formidable size and variety of resources. Whether or not diplomatic relations between Washington and Hanoi are established and even if Vietnam receives American economic aid, this will not deflect the Lao Dong leaders from their ultimate goals, whatever those are.

Even without subversive interference in the domestic affairs of its neighbors—which the ASEAN countries currently dread—or direct military intervention in the region—for which it has the capability but not necessarily the intention—Vietnam is and will remain the Southeast Asian model and symbol of successful revolution. It will be a constant and increasingly vocal reminder that there are alternatives to cooperation with the industrial democracies for countries eager to overcome social and economic backwardness.

The Sino-Soviet conflict may create some serious complications for the Lao Dong leaders. The Chinese might fear that a hegemonial Vietnam, leading a Southeast Asian Federation which could have 478 million inhabitants by 1990, might become a Soviet ally and place the Chinese People's Republic between the strategic pincers of two powerful military partners. Peking might choose either to prevent Vietnamese expansion or to encourage Hanoi to pursue its "manifest destiny" without excessive dependence on the Soviet Union, by providing enough support to balance Moscow's influence. How the Chinese could effectively prevent the Vietnamese from carrying out hegemonial aspirations is not easy to imagine, especially if the Russians were prepared to help. The Chinese might eventually be compelled to assist—in competition with the Russians—Vietnam to become a third Communist great power, to induce it to maintain an equidistant uncommitted position between the Soviet Union and the People's Republic.

Of course, it is by no means established that the Lao Dong leaders have decided on a forward movement in Southeast Asia or that they will so decide in the future. There is a long way from ideologically combative newspaper editorials and radio broadcasts to the commitment of material resources for the implementation of an adventurist foreign policy. Vietnam might reduce the readiness of its forces only to the level its leaders consider necessary for defense, while maximum priority is given to national reconstruction and development. If Vietnam were to choose the peaceful road, it would have nothing to fear from its neighbors at least through the 1980s. On the Southeast Asian mainland, Thailand is the only country equal in population to Vietnam. Its recent governments have been weak, and it has been plagued by local insurgencies for many years. Its armed forces are no match for PAVN and could under no conceivable circumstances initiate armed conflict. As mentioned earlier, the PAVN probably exceeds by a substantial margin the forces deployed by the People's Republic of China in the military regions close to Vietnam. In a defensive mode, PAVN would prevail over the People's Liberation Army (PLA) forces China could afford to commit to a campaign in the South, without redeploying forces dedicated to the protection of vital assets against the Soviet forces positioned along the Sino-Soviet border.

Were a major Sino-Soviet war to occur, Vietnam would risk attack from China only if it became an ally of the Soviet Union. Alternatively, assuming future Sino-Soviet reconciliation, Southeast Asia would then cease being an area of strategic contention between the two Communist powers. A peaceful and nonaligned Vietnam would probably not become a target of Chinese aggression for expansionist purposes in the 1980s.

This leaves only a militaristic Indonesia as a possible threat to Vietnam in the time frame of the 1980s. The question has been raised in many circles, since the end of the war in Indochina, whether Vietnam and Indonesia, or Communist Indochina and ASEAN, are likely eventually to find themselves on a collision course.

The present regimes in Vietnam and Indonesia are indeed ideological adversaries who have each won a decisive victory

NATIONAL POLITICS AND REGIONAL POWERS

against their internal enemies. Although neither government has articulated explicit claims to spheres of influence, they may have overlapping but antagonistic interests in the political evolution of Thailand and Malaysia. Were the Indonesian armed forces to have the capability to come to the support of Thailand in case of a Vietnamese military intervention in a Thai civil war, open warfare between Vietnam and Indonesia would not be inconceivable. But as long as Vietnam and Indonesia devote their energies and resources to their respective national development, their ideological antagonism will not necessarily lead to armed confrontation. A generation ago, Walter Lippmann compared the United States as a sea power to a whale and the Soviet Union as a land power to an elephant and concluded that if each stayed in its natural element they would have no reason to fight and that if they decided to fight the aggressor would be at a disadvantage.

The allegory applies to Vietnam and Indonesia within the boundaries of Southeast Asia. If Indonesia decides to overcome its current military weakness, it could assume the role and responsibilities of a regional maritime power. As a country consisting of 13,000 islands and claiming control under the archipelago concept of the waters surrounding its territory, Indonesia needs a navy and will certainly acquire a maritime capability when its economic resources make this possible. Vietnam could become a hegemonial power on the Southeast Asian mainland if it maintained superior land and air forces, whereas its interests in the South China Sea are limited to the defense of its long coast and do not require a blue-water navy. Vietnam is not likely to invest heavily in naval power in pursuit of its moot claim to the Spratly Islands and the Paracels against competing claims by China. Rational defense planners in Hanoi are bound to devote available resources to the maintenance of strong land and air forces in defense of Vietnam's only land threat, China, and in pursuit of its own political aspirations on the mainland of Southeast Asia.

At a later stage of industrial development beyond the 1980s, a Vietnam successful in establishing hegemony over its immediate neighbors might also seek to acquire naval power. But, if the more forboding speculations presented earlier do not materialize and, if ideological antagonisms subside, it is conceivable that Vietnam

73

DIVERSITY AND DEVELOPMENT IN SOUTHEAST ASIA

would become the protector of Southeast Asia against pressures from its giant continental neighbors, China and India. Meanwhile, Indonesia could play a similar role in securing the region from the unwanted interference of the global maritime powers, the Soviet Union and the United States. Thus the hope of the smaller countries of Southeast Asia for a zone of peace, freedom, and neutrality would be fulfilled. But relations between Vietnam and the ASEAN countries will not become friendly as long as their regional cold war continues. At present Vietnam is militantly communist and all five ASEAN countries pursue harsh anticommunist policies. Under the circumstances, cooperation between the two camps seems unlikely, and it is difficult to visualize a relaxation of tensions without changes of regime or at least reduced ideological militancy on either or both sides.

FIVE

The North-South Conflict

The various minor ethnic or territorial conflicts that could occur in the next 15 years between neighboring Southeast Asian states were not examined in detail, because it does not seem likely that Balkan-style wars will be caused by currently dormant disputes such as Philippine claims to Sabah, Malaysian claims to the Muslim parts of Thailand, Laotian claims to territories south of the Mekong, or other such irredentist claims that could be brought to life by nationalists with antiquarian emotions or anthropological inclinations.

More likely than any such atavistic sources of troublemaking is a paradigmatic change of perspective that would render present ideological rivalries or power plays obsolete because of the growing importance of the more basic global conflict between rich and poor countries. Romantic nationalist escapades such as Sukarno's "confrontation" with Malaysia, or minor-league ideological cold wars between ASEAN and Indochina, are hardly relevant to the solution of the enormously difficult problems facing the countries which came late to the Industrial Revolution and attribute their misfortunes to past colonialism and present exploitation by the advanced industrial democracies.

The grievances of Third World countries are very similar in Latin America, Africa, and Asia. In the United Nations, especially through the Group of 77, in which the Southeast Asian states have been active participants and which now has some 113 members, and in many other special gatherings, the developing countries have frequent opportunities to exchange views, educate each other, and standardize the concepts and the terminology they use in communicating their point of view. The states of Southeast Asia share with the other Third World nations the painful memories left by the age of Western dominance. As exporters of natural resources they have been, both in the colonial past and since independence, subject to the often unbeneficial vagaries of the world market. As the result of their economies' dependence on a few minerals or cash crops, they have repeatedly had the experience of seeing the benefits of capital transfers in the form of economic aid nullified by the drop in the price of their main exports on the world market.

As exporters of commodities who believe, rightly or wrongly, that long-term trends in the terms of trade have habitually favored the industrial countries to their detriment, the countries of Southeast Asia are understandably interested in participating in the creation of the New International Economic Order from which the Third World expects a correction of what they perceive as past injustices. The questions that seem to deserve special attention with regard to Southeast Asia are not the global issues of the North-South conflict but rather what specific contributions that particular group of countries could make to the common cause of the Third World.

It is an interesting question whether, despite their ideological differences, the ASEAN countries, Indochina, and isolationist Burma have a common interest in a New International Economic Order and whether that common bond will eventually override present differences and forge a regional entity which will act jointly in the world arena against the industrial democracies, in coordination with similar groupings from other parts of the world. Professor Frank Golay doubts that Southeast Asia will act as a regional entity in the North-South confrontation. I am inclined to believe that the conflict between industrial and developing countries—if it lasts several more years and generates much rancor—could become a unifying bond within the region, despite local territorial contests and ideological antagonisms.

The feelings of inferiority left in all of the Third World by four and a half centuries of Western dominance, which its beneficiaries justified in terms of racial and cultural superiority, and the moral indignation which is still driving the ex-colonial victims of personal abuse and economic deprivation are dynamic factors of considerable intensity in the sharpening confrontation between the Third World and the industrial democracies.

Despite their own expansionist record, the Russians and the Chinese do not arouse the same ire in the Third World. The contiguity of their annexations made it possible for Russia and China to absorb the conquered nationalities into multinational states in which, in principle at least, all ethnic and linguistic groups are treated as equals. As none of the nationalities conquered by the Russians or the Chinese have become independent states, unlike the former colonies of the West, their voices are not heard at the gatherings of the Third World. As countries with centrally planned economies and socialist state systems, the Soviet Union and the People's Republic of China also have the advantage of being dissociated from the image of capitalist exploitation and manipulation of world market prices, despite the fact that in concrete instances Soviet and Chinese state representatives are themselves very tough bargainers when purchasing natural resources from the Third World. Although their ideological influence is feared and their subversive potential is perhaps overestimated, the Soviet Union and the People's Republic of China are not perceived as adversaries by the South. This situation might generate perplexing ambivalences and perhaps new alignments among the countries of Southeast Asia. Regardless of their own ideological orientation, the Southeast Asians are all anxious to keep to a minimum the interference of the major powers in the affairs of the region, but they are also interested in securing allies against the industrial democracies, especially if it appears that there will be no easy resolution of the North-South conflict in the near future.

The economic dimensions of the North-South conflict have been explored in greater detail than either the moral-psychological or the political ones. Little can be added here on the economic issues involved. The success of the Organization of Petroleum Exporting Countries (OPEC) in increasing the price of crude oil fourfold after October 1973 has triggered interest in similar cartels for the control of the supply and prices of other natural resources. The prospects for such cartels have been discussed by Professor Uri Azad in his paper for the 1980s Project.[17] What role, however, would Southeast Asia play in such arrangements? The data supplied by Professor Azad indicate that Southeast Asia is not a significant repository of mineral reserves, with the exception of tin, of which Thailand, Malaysia, and Indonesia hold 61.1 percent of known global reserves.[18] However, according to the same source, expected demand growth is only 1.2 percent per year and substitution and conservation possibilities for tin are good. Obviously, lack of access to Southeast Asian tin would not affect the industrial democracies in any significant way.

It was mentioned earlier that Indonesia has at best 2.1 percent of the world's proven crude oil reserves. In 1974 its production was 2.6 percent of the total global oil production, with a daily production rate of 1.4 million barrels, placing Indonesia in twelfth place. As the only important oil producer in Southeast Asia, Indonesia was a major beneficiary of OPEC price increases, but Indonesian influence on the cartel was minor, its production amounting to only 5.7 percent of that of the Middle East and North Africa.[19] Tropical agricultural products, such as rubber, sugar, coffee, and tea, of which Southeast Asia is an important producer, would also not give the region significant market leverage, because either substitution possibilities are available to the industrial democracies or production could be expanded in other parts of the tropical world where neither land nor labor are at this time serious constraints on supply.[20]

Professor Frank Golay reached the conclusion that objective conditions and rational economic analysis will deter the ASEAN countries from endorsing the more radical positions of the Group of 77 in its confrontation with the industrial democracies. I disa-

[17]Uri Azad, "Scarce Natural Resources and Armed Conflict in the Late 1980s," the 1980s Project. (Mimeographed.) This essay will appear in a forthcoming volume on natural resources published by McGraw-Hill Book Company, New York.
[18]Ibid., pp. 32–33.
[19]Carlson, *Indonesia's Oil*, p. 21.
[20]The Brookings Institution, *Trade in Primary Commodities: Conflict or Cooperation*, Washington, D.C., 1974. p. 18.

gree with this conclusion. Professor Widjojo and other members of the Indonesian cabinet told me in Jakarta in June 1976 that President Suharto had decided that Indonesia should play an active role in the North-South confrontation. Positions taken by Indonesian representatives at international gatherings since then confirm this information. If one assumes that the Third World will fail to obtain indexed prices for their raw materials, debt rescheduling, increased capital transfers on concessional terms, and free access to advanced technology, the policies supporting these objectives would be irrational as seen from Professor Golay's perspective. But Presidents Suharto and Marcos are supporting these objectives, apparently in the belief that the South can "win" and that, accordingly, Indonesia and the Philippines will benefit.

Because of its economic weakness, the Third World can prevail in its attempt to restructure the global economic system only by an act of collective political will and consistent solidarity in bargaining with the industrial democracies. By now this is widely understood by Third World leaders. They view their many gatherings as a continuing process of political organization, comparable to the development of Western trade unionism in the wake of the Industrial Revolution.

The future role of Southeast Asia in the North-South conflict will be determined by politics rather than by economics. Southeast Asia does not have economic leverage over the industrial democracies. It needs their markets, equipment, skills, and capital in order to stay ahead of population growth and to achieve some real economic development. Yet the urge for political vindication is likely to prevail. The countries of the region share the characteristic moral and psychological reactions to colonialism. The spokesmen for the Third World are being caught by the inherent momentum of their rhetoric. As the industrial democracies do not respond to their demands, the tone of the debate gets sharper. The political and emotional costs of backing down lead to further hardening of positions. Yielding to the dictates of economic rationality is particularly difficult in international disputes with strong nationalist overtones. The 1974 and 1975 special sessions of the UN General Assembly offer a case in point.

At the Sixth Special Session of the UN General Assembly held in April 1974, the four ASEAN members who participated in the general debate—Indonesia, Malaysia, the Philippines, and Thailand—adopted markedly less radical positions than President Houari Boumedienne of Algeria, who, as chairman of the nonaligned countries, had been instructed to request the Special Session. In his keynote address, Boumedienne demanded nationalization of all natural resources under the sovereignty of Third World countries, with technical help from the United Nations for their continued exploitation and commercialization, price-fixing cartels for all commodities, and high-speed industrialization with substantial aid from the developed world. All ASEAN countries tacitly rejected these proposals by ignoring them in their speeches, although all complained about unfair terms of trade, the slackening in the pace of international development, the protectionism of the industrial powers, and the balance-of-payments problems created by the increase in the price of oil and of their imports.

Unlike the Algerian president, who advocated nationalization of all natural resources and global cartels in line with his country's socialist policies, the remedies proposed by Malaysia were congruent with the interests of an economy directed by market forces and a social system dominated by foreign and domestic capital, namely commodity agreements based on "reference prices which should be acceptable to both producer and consumer countries and realistic enough to take into account such factors as the supply and demand position, the changes in currency parities, inflation, and the development needs of the developing countries."[21]

The Thai delegation voiced similar complaints in the course of reciting its government's concern about rising oil costs, "unfair and noncommercial competition by rich [rice] producers for its traditional markets," and trade deficits, which were expected to reach $680 million for that year.[22] Like his ASEAN colleagues, the Thai representative did not endorse revolutionary proposals, concluding only that "it is apparent that necessary adjustments which are long overdue in the economic sphere must be made to

[21] UN General Assembly, *Document A/PV.2222*, 23 April 1974, p. 26.
[22] UN General Assembly, *Document A/PV.2220*, 19 April 1974, p. 46.

resolve the present crisis and to avert future catastrophes." The only two items of the proposed action program which the Thai delegation endorsed explicitly were "the establishment of a link between prices of raw materials and primary commodities exported by developing countries and the manufactured and semi-manufactured goods and capital equipment imported by them" and the provision that "the export markets for food products of developing countries should be ensured through just and equitable arrangements, *inter alia* by the elimination of unfair competition, to protect the poor, developing countries that export food products from non-commercial practices of the developed countries."[23] In other words, Thailand was interested primarily in price indexation and in the elimination of United States rice sales on concessional terms under the P.L. 480 program, which affects its export markets. But like the other ASEAN countries, having an economy linked primarily to the industrial democracies and an economic system based on free-market forces and private capital, Thailand was not interested in a radical restructuring of the global economy.

Indonesia, in turn, as an oil-exporting country, told the industrial democracies that they cannot expect "the developing oil-producing countries [to] continue to subsidize the industrialization of the advanced countries,"[24] but the general tenor of Foreign Minister Adam Malik's remarks was conciliatory.

All Southeast Asian countries which were members of the United Nations—Burma, Indonesia, the Khmer Republic, Laos, Malaysia, the Philippines, Singapore, and Thailand—cosponsored the "Declaration on the Establishment of a New International Economic Order" and the "Programme of Action" that the Sixth Special Session of the UN General Assembly adopted on May 2, 1974.[25] But the ASEAN countries who participated in the general debate urged cooperation with the industrial powers, shunned provocative statements, and did not advocate radical measures in their speeches.

At the August 1975, Fifth Conference of Foreign Ministers of

[23]Ibid., p. 57.
[24]UN General Assembly, *Document A/PV.2214*, 15 April 1974, p. 53.
[25]UN General Assembly, *Document A/9556* (Part II), 1 May 1974.

Non-aligned Countries, held in Peru, a militant "Lima Program for International Assistance and Solidarity" was adopted. Although the atmosphere was more militant than it had been the previous year at the United Nations, Foreign Minister Adam Malik of Indonesia commented favorably on the change of position of the United States government following an unsuccessful preparatory meeting in April 1975 in Paris which had been unable to agree on the agenda for a Conference on International Economic Cooperation (CIEC).[26]

In a speech in Kansas City on May 13, 1975, Secretary of State Henry A. Kissinger had reversed American opposition to the inclusion of nonenergy issues with the result that the CIEC was held in Paris in December 1975 and four commissions were established—for energy, raw materials, development, and finance—to conduct a "multilateral economic dialogue." Indonesia was the only member of ASEAN among the 27 countries involved in this new departure in international economic diplomacy.

Following the Seventh Special Session of the UN General Assembly, the CIEC meetings in Paris, the discussion of the Group of 77 in preparation for the Fourth UN Conference on Trade and Development (UNCTAD) in Nairobi, OPEC consultations, and many other exchanges of views among Third World countries, Indonesia and the Philippines have abandoned their conciliatory position in the North-South conflict in favor of more militant policies. The reasons for this change of policy were explained to me in June 1976 in Jakarta by Professor Widjojo Nitisastro. As intellectual leader of an American-educated group of faculty members from the School of Economics of the University of Indonesia, he has played an important role in assisting President Suharto in developing the economic policies which rescued the Indonesian economy from the hyperinflation of the 1960s. These policies gave free-market forces considerable rein, created an extremely favorable climate for private foreign in-

---

[26] Address by Foreign Minister Adam Malik of Indonesia at the Conference of Foreign Ministers of Non-aligned Countries, Lima, Peru, 25–29 August 1975, p. 17. (Mimeographed.)

vestments, and produced development plans which received the full support of the World Bank and of the International Monetary Fund.

After following a moderating role at Third World meetings for several years, the Indonesian government had reached the conclusion that its interests as a commodity-exporting country required that it should participate more actively in the North-South dialogue to strike a better balance between Third World political solidarity and the pursuit of national short-term economic gains. Indonesia is now fully supporting the common goals spelled out in the Manila Declaration of February 1976, including indexation of raw materials prices, debt rescheduling, increased aid on concessional terms, preferential tariffs for the import of manufactured goods from developing to advanced countries, and unrestricted technology transfers.

Professor Widjojo and his colleagues were pleased that the Group of 77 stayed together through the Fourth Session of UNCTAD in Nairobi in May 1976, adhering to the carefully prepared common positions worked out in regional Asian, African, and Latin American special sessions which were embodied in the very important Manila Declaration. The industrial democracies, on the other hand, seemed unprepared and unable to agree on a common position. Third World countries at Nairobi felt that their carefully developed proposals for an integrated commodities program had not been seriously studied by the Organization of Economic Cooperation and Development (OECD) group and that American counterproposals were diversified and ignored the fact that for the Third World the problem is one of prices and markets, not of investments and supplies.

At all Third World meetings there is now growing consciousness about the importance of economic cooperation among developing countries through financial arrangements and exchange of experience. Indonesia, Professor Widjojo claimed, is consulted by other Third World countries on debt rescheduling, production sharing in the oil industry, and access to Western capital markets, as part of a growing effort to coordinate policies.

The next major episode in the process of Third World political mobilization was the fifth nonaligned summit conference held in

August 1976 in Colombo, Sri Lanka. The Economic Declaration adopted by 86 countries states:

The heads of state or government of the non-aligned countries are strongly convinced that any solution which does not contain a complete reconstruction of international economic relations by way of introducing a new international economic system will not contribute to placing the developing countries in the position in which an acceptable degree of development can be reached. They confirm their determination to continue making joint efforts aimed at realizing these goals, particularly by way of forming associations of producers, as well as by way of other means, despite threats and repressive economic sanctions.[27]

The full texts, totaling more than 40,000 words, deserve close scrutiny. They appear to be a first major step toward the achievement of collective economic self-reliance by Third World countries. The participants made serious efforts to find technically feasible joint projects for self-help and to create better bargaining positions in the North-South dialogue.

Meanwhile, the industrial democracies persisted throughout 1976 in what to the Third World appeared as dilatory tactics. They made proposals at the United Nations which were not supported by the political will to implement them and treated the CIEC discussions in Paris as leisurely "experiments in international economic diplomacy." It was only at the end of May 1977, at the ministerial meeting of the CIEC in Paris, that the new spirit in which the Carter Administration views the North-South dialogue was publicly expressed in the proposals presented by Secretary of State Cyrus R. Vance, who stated: "There must be a new international economic system. In that system there must be equity; there must be growth; but, above all, there must be justice. We are prepared to help build that new system."[28] Although the public reaction of some Third World representatives was cool, criticizing as inadequate the package of economic concessions offered by the United States,[29] Professor Widjojo,

[27]*FBIS, Middle East and North Africa,* No. 164, 23 August 1976, p. AA5.
[28]Department of State, Bureau of Public Affairs, Speech by Secretary of State Cyrus R. Vance, Paris, May 30, 1977.
[29]Paul Lewis, "Poor Countries Cool to Offer by the Rich," *The New York Times,* June 1, 1977.

whom I saw again in Jakarta a few days after his return from Paris, felt that progress was being made and viewed the forthcoming rounds of negotiations more optimistically than during our conversation a year earlier.

Southeast Asia's noncommunist governments and elites justify their existence in part by their capacity to cooperate with the industrial democracies. They essentially want to remain within the global capitalist system, but this increasingly discredits them in the eyes of their nations' youth. They are anxious for help from the industrial democracies to achieve economic growth more rapidly through benign policies because they realize that, unless they succeed in that task and prove to the masses that they can provide social justice, their present systems of government are doomed.

The spirit of revolt stirring the Third World is not likely to subside or vanish unless the international community provides practical solutions to the North-South problem. The means by which the industrial democracies secured the survival of friendly regimes in most of Southeast Asia after 1945 are no longer adequate. Without bold new methods of international cooperation the present noncommunist Southeast Asian governments will be displaced within the next decade by radicals who may reject "collective bargaining" and opt for some form of international "class war" of the poor countries against the rich.

National Economic Priorities and International Coalitions

Frank H. Golay

ONE

Perspective on the Region

Southeast Asian states have impeccable credentials for membership in Southern councils; they are tropical, they share a colonial past, they are integrated with the rest of the world as producers of primary products, and they provide a relatively low level of material well-being for their inhabitants.[1]

Behind the voice of this world region in the North-South confrontation will be found those factors that determine the interest of each component state in the goals sought by the Group of 77. The intensity of this interest will reflect policies and institutions evolved by the society to pursue economic goals, the benefits and costs attributed by the society to participation in the existing economic order of trade and payments, and the success with which the economy meets the material needs of the society.

It is also necessary to consider the likelihood that the voice of Southeast Asia will be amplified by regional cohesion, that the collective voice will be more strident than the sum of the voices of

[1]The definition of Southeast Asia remains fluid despite the quarter-century of independent existence of the states of the area. In some cases, the region is considered to embrace Taiwan and Hong Kong to the northeast. For other purposes, Sri Lanka and Bangladesh and even the larger states of the Indian subcontinent to the west and north are included. Over time, however, a substantial and growing consensus has emerged which specifies Southeast Asia as the arc of states stretching from Burma on the northwest to the Philippines on the northeast and including Burma, Malaysia, Singapore, Brunei, Indonesia, Thailand, Cambodia, Laos, Vietnam, and the Philippines. This concept of Southeast Asia will be used herein.

the component states. The answer to this question will hinge upon those features of the Southeast Asian environment which determine the strength of regionalism.

Common to the states of Southeast Asia is a strategy of national development designed to ensure that a preponderance of the benefits accrue to members of the national society rather than development unconcerned with the nationality of its beneficiaries. National development is distinguished by intervention of the state in economic processes to enable nationals to preempt the rewarding roles provided by growth, by policies designed to transfer ownership and control of modern economic activities to members of the national society, and by efforts to restructure the economy by forcing the growth of the manufacturing sector. The preoccupation of Southeast Asian societies with these national dimensions of development has served to perpetuate the economic isolation of state from state which distinguished colonial development and has nurtured powerful interests inimical to the pooling of national interests with those of other societies in the region. Although regional initiatives and interactions will proliferate in the future as they have in the past, in the absence of a strong base of economic integration there is little likelihood that the interests common to the societies in the area will be capable of submerging the underlying separateness of Southeast Asian states.

THE CONTOURS OF SOUTHEAST ASIA

Southeast Asia is, and will remain for years to come, a crazy quilt of diversity—cultural, racial, ethnic, religious, political, and economic. The basic racial stocks as diluted by migrant racial elements contribute to diversity as does the ethnic and linguistic fragmentation attributable to geographic configuration and topography, as well as a long history of tensions and warfare which have redistributed and mixed the peoples of the region. Diversity also has resulted from the importation of competing religions: Buddhism and Hinduism from the Indian subcontinent, Taoism and ancestor worship from China, Islam from the Middle East via

Gujarat, and Christianity from northwestern Europe. Diversity also reflects such factors as the timing and motivation of the Western penetration, the economic and political organization of colonies within the capabilities of the colonial powers, and the intellectual and ideological ferment in the West within which colonial policies and practices evolved.

The states of Southeast Asia must live with the reality of their smallness: not in terms of population, as Indonesia is the fifth most populous country in the world, and not necessarily in terms of area, as most of the states in the region fall in the middle range among countries. With the exception of Vietnam, and possibly also of Indonesia, they must be assessed as "small" in terms of dimensions of strength which can be mobilized to ensure their continued existence as independent states. States relatively small in terms of power have few external options, and the foreign policies of such states tend to be distinguished by historical continuity.[2] Over the longer haul, the states of Southeast Asia formed out of the basins of the south-flowing Irrawaddy, Salween, Chao Phraya, and Mekong rivers must seek autonomous existence as buffers between more powerful states. The Philippines, Malaysia, and Singapore, creations of Western colonialism with shallow roots in history, will continue to recognize the need to cultivate powerful patrons within and without the region of East Asia. Vietnam and Indonesia, embodying more impressive dimensions of strength and with self-confidence deeply rooted in history, will exercise greater independence of action, but they too will be constrained by environmental realities.

Since the demise of colonialism, representative government in the region has led a precarious existence. Initial faith in the cohesiveness and shared purpose of societies freed of the colonial "yoke" was reflected in the installation of parliamentary governments and the organization of political competition through

[2]The validity of this observation has been obscured by four decades of warfare and accelerated change attending the liquidation of Western colonialism in the region. Southeast Asia has a rich history of some 10 centuries of meaningful political organization which confirms the basic pattern of foreign relations imposed by the organization of the region into relatively small and relatively autonomous political units.

parties. Today, in Burma, Indonesia, and Thailand, government is in the hands of military elites, dissent is vigorously suppressed, and moves to reactivate representative government are nonexistent or halting. Monolithic governments are strongly entrenched in Vietnam, Laos, and Cambodia. Malaysia and Singapore have representative governments, but openness is limited and authoritarian policies control areas of vital concern to the dominant racial group in each of these states. Internal ferment in Thailand, which boiled over in violence in the fall of 1973 and swept from power the last in a succession of governments dominated by the military bureaucracy which ruled for four decades, erupted once again in the fall of 1976 and toppled a parliamentary government which had survived for three precarious years. In the Philippines, Ferdinand Marcos, an incumbent lame-duck president, chose five years ago to hold onto power by declaring martial law. Congress has been prorogued and a vigorous, critical press silenced, and Marcos rules by decree. Although martial law as an emergency measure was sanctioned by the existing constitution, there is little evidence that Marcos has plans to revive representative government.

The governments of the area are highly centralized, and in a number of cases power resides in one person. But all leaders are mortal, and the consequences of changes in leadership for domestic and regional political stability cannot be predicted with confidence. In the Indochinese states, Thailand, and Malaysia, changes in leadership, in and of themselves, are unlikely to tax seriously the existing stability. In Burma, Indonesia, and the Philippines, where political power is personal and authoritarian, the problem of the succession to power is ignored by the present leadership. In these states, changes in leadership are likely to be associated with some confusion and instability.

The threshold of recognition of external economic policy issues and options is high among members of Southeast Asian societies generally. Political leaders of the area are relatively free, therefore, to articulate the foreign economic policies of the societies they represent without jeopardizing their leadership. Because the world views of all but a few members of the societies for which they speak are vague and undifferentiated, they are assured that they can mobilize internal support with nationalistic and simplistic slogans. The obvious economic interests behind the South's confrontation with the North are buttressed by a uniform image of colonial and neocolonial "exploitation" which is shared by Southeast Asians. Because this is the case, a militant stance on North-South issues will not be challenged but will serve to mobilize support behind leaders advocating such militancy. The failure of a Southeast Asian leader to articulate such a position would be exceedingly irrational from the point of view of his own interests.

The economies of Southeast Asia differ widely in capabilities and orientation. The most affluent and rapidly growing economy in the area is the city-state of Singapore. Industrialization has proceeded rapidly, and Singapore's *entrepôt* trade and the provision of services to shipping have declined in importance relative to the value added to a wide range of manufactured products by Singapore's skilled and efficient labor force. Its economy has been disciplined by exposure to outside competition and is supported by sophisticated credit and capital market institutions.

At the other extreme, Burma, reflecting historical tradition and geographic realities, has turned in on itself to seek a unique Burmese future independent of its neighbors and the wider world. The variety and volume of its international economic and political exchanges have contracted, and isolation remains a priority interest of the ruling military elite. Burma's neighbors to the east and west appear satisfied to have Burma as a buffer, and the Soviet Union and the United States presently appear to have no major interest in that remote corner of the world. The Burmese leadership has extended Burmese isolation to international organizations, and this situation is unlikely to change radically over the next decade.[3]

Fragmentary information from Cambodia and Laos suggests that the leaders of these societies are pursuing economic and political modernization through variants of agrarian-based com-

---

[3]In recent years, Burma has experienced a collapse in its capability to mobilize an export surplus of rice which has precipitated a severe balance-of-payments crisis. To deal with this problem, Burma has turned to international lending agencies and, more tentatively, to economic aid sources to maintain minimum levels of imports. Whether or not these developments signal a durable change in the "Burmese Way to Socialism" remains to be seen.

munism influenced by the mainland Chinese experience. These states, as communist societies generally, are not likely to pursue development based on international specialization and inter-dependence with the outside world, particularly the capitalist world. If Cambodia and Laos choose to participate in the Group of 77, they can be expected to support radical initiatives but from political rather than economic motives.

Vietnam is an unknown "quantity" in contemplating the future of the region. The traditional communist interest in economic independence suggests that a unified Vietnam will be relatively indifferent to the economic benefits to be gained from the North-South confrontation. This assessment is supported by the com-plementarity of the economies of northern and southern Vietnam and the need to rehabilitate the war damage in the south and to integrate the population of that area into the larger national soci-ety. The self-confidence of the northern Vietnamese, however, may cause them to pursue political interests in Southeast Asia. Similarly, they may find it in their interest to seek influence in the Group of 77. To predict at this point that Vietnam will provide initiatives—or ignore outside initiatives—toward Southeast Asian regionalism or Southern solidarity can be little more than speculation.

The remaining states of the area, Malaysia, Brunei, Indonesia, Thailand, and the Philippines, have important economic charac-teristics in common.[4] They are open economies integrated with the outside world, and they maintain extensive scope for indi-vidualism in organizing production. At the same time, they are mixed economies in which government intervention in economic processes with direct controls, public financial institutions, and diverse state enterprises is extensive. The economic roles of government in these states do not reflect a commitment to mar-kets, competition, and efficiency so much as they reflect a prefer-ence for control and regulation of economic activities to pursue those national interests identified by the elites exercising power.

---

[4]Brunei, a small oil-rich enclave on the west coast of Borneo, is lumped with the open economies of the region. No attempt will be made to extend the analysis of particular countries of the area to Brunei.

These states are serious in their efforts to improve the performance of economic policies and institutions—fiscal systems, social services, the infrastructure of social capital, the banking system, economic planning, rural development, credit cooperatives, and so forth—within the context of the existing mixed economy. The success of these efforts varies widely within governments and among countries.

Each of these states presently behaves as if the gains to be realized from specialization and trade are substantial. This is not to say that they seek to maximize trade and interdependence; they seek expanded trade subject to the constraints arising in the competition among goals which contribute to the social welfare of a society. High priority will be maintained for export expansion, however, by the imbalance in external payments which inevitably attends efforts to accelerate economic growth. Similarly, these states behave as if direct foreign investment can be used to augment indigenous resources in short supply, and their leaders seek foreign investment subject to conditions which they believe will protect adequately the interests of the host society.

The interests of the states of Southeast Asia in the potential gains from the North-South confrontation will have to vie with the range of clamorous priorities which compete for the attention of the leaders of these societies. Because these states are relatively weak and the external environment uncertain and volatile, Southeast Asian leaders can be expected to remain preoccupied with security interests through the 1980s. This concern will be manifested in many areas, not the least of which will be the range of policies designed to reduce the tensions arising in linguistic, ethnic, racial, and class differences which have limited national integration.

The boundaries of Southeast Asian states and the diverse populations within those boundaries reflect historical accident rather than internal logic. Throughout its independent existence, Burma has been divided by the aspirations for national independence of the Karens, Shans, Chins, and Kachins and their resentment of Burman political dominance. Malaysia cannot escape the divisive tensions of communalism rooted in the rough numerical balance between the politically dominant Malay community and the economically dominant Chinese community. In Indonesia, Javanese hegemony has not been accepted passively in the Outer Islands, which provided the leadership, labor, and economic resources behind the rebellion in 1958. In the southern Philippines, Muslim communities are fighting for the right to secede and thereby escape the dominance of the Christian Filipinos. Resentment of the influence of the southern Tagalogs in national politics is also widespread in that country. Today, the festering pockets of dissidence centered in ethnic, religious, and national minorities scattered through the areas peripheral to the central plain of Thailand demand the attention of that country's leaders.

Functional specialization has also contributed to the fragmentation of Southeast Asian societies. As is well known, Asian aliens dominated retail trade and the assembly of small-holder export crops and, by so doing, remained distinctive and resented by indigenous members of these societies. Regional loyalties and interests also reflect intracountry agricultural specialization arising in distinctive climatic regimes and varied soil endowments and the enclave development of dispersed mineral and forest resources.

National integration is pursued by diverse permutations and combinations of repression and cooptation. Pressures on aliens to assimilate are maintained by immigration and naturalization policies and administrative discretion in their implementation, regulation of access to economic activities and resources, and discretionary administration of incentives and subsidies. Efforts to structure national education systems that promise to reduce the divisiveness of ethnic and linguistic pluralism are universal, as are policies to disperse governmental services, social investment, industrial activity, and employment. Although gaps between announced plans and accomplishments persist, concern for national integration is prominent in each state within the region.

The foregoing generalizations about Southeast Asia are more or less valid when applied to the various states in the region. As they are extrapolated into the future, their reliability becomes less certain. The fighting stopped in Vietnam two years ago, and the future relations among the states of the area and the wider international relations of the region are pregnant with uncertainty.

TWO

Economic Goals and Strategies

Political leaders of the open economies in Southeast Asia recognize a stake in maintaining the economic growth rates which have prevailed in the area in recent years. Malaysia, the Philippines, Thailand, and Singapore have experienced growth in aggregate output in the range of 5 percent per year, the target rate of the United Nations Development Decade of the 1960s. Indonesia has made considerable progress in overcoming the economic dislocation of the period of Guided Democracy. Average savings ratios are increasing slowly, and marginal rates maintained by some of the countries promise continued improvement. Growth in export earnings has been maintained at encouraging levels, and ratios of tax revenues to aggregate income, while low by Western standards, are increasing generally.

These sketchy and impressionistic generalizations are not to say that the open economies of the area have "taken off," but to suggest that leaders of these states recognize that the growth rates of the past decade are a necessary—but not sufficient—condition for their retention of power without intensifying repression. They are aware that expectations of steady growth have been created by sustained discussion of economic development, and they are confident that if they are successful in maintaining current rates of growth, the likelihood of continued social stability will be markedly improved.

Pursuit of this goal is certain to maintain heavy pressure on available foreign exchange resources. The expansion in export earnings which will take place over the next decade and a half, however, is unlikely to provide sufficient foreign exchange to import capital equipment and inputs required by manufacturing expansion, to service foreign borrowings, official and private, and to meet the cruel increase in the cost of imported fuel supplies.

The political leaders of Southeast Asia cannot escape pressures to speed the pace of industrialization. Concern for this goal reflects the priorities assigned to economic growth, expanded employment opportunities outside agriculture, qualitative improvement in human resources, trade diversification, and so forth, as well as more general considerations of security and national survival. Industrial strategies range widely in proximate goals but in general are based upon the internal market and are implemented by powerful incentives in the form of protection, tax remission, subsidized credit, and preferential tax treatment for investment expenditures. In the distribution of these incentives preference is given to nationals of the country concerned.

Despite the priority maintained for industrial development, progress toward this goal has remained modest, and the structures of the Southeast Asian economies have changed slowly over the past quarter-century. Manufacturing is high-cost and relatively inefficient except for the limited processing of export commodities. Bias toward scale characterizes industrialization as manufacturing enterprises have tended to materialize full-blown and of considerable scale as entrepreneurs are recruited from existing political elites. Such individuals have knowledge of the incentives, the political "clout" to influence their allocation, and access to savings and credit resources required to bring the proposed enterprise to fruition. Scale bias also results because administrators of industrialization policies prefer to deal with a few relatively large projects rather than face the difficulties of administering many small projects. The industrial structure is further distorted by the concentration of production around the capital city where political decisions are made and financial resources, technical expertise, and the principal domestic market for manufactures are found.

Pressures to speed industrialization are matched by the need to expand food supplies to keep pace with the region's rapid population growth. Urban populations are relatively sophisticated and volatile, particularly those of the dominant capital cities, and political leaders recognize their stake in an easy food supply which keeps bellies filled and is a major factor in dampening inflationary pressures. Thanks to the new technologies promising major increases in yields and bilateral and multilateral aid funds for agricultural development, Southeast Asian governments are applying an increasing proportion of available resources to food production. All of the states of the region are capable of maintaining present levels of per capita food absorption through the 1980s. They will do so by applying more inputs and new techniques in the domestic agricultural sector or, where necessary, by allocating available foreign exchange to import foodstuffs.

Although control of population is not a concern of comparable importance to Southeast Asian societies, it is gaining in importance. The success of international, national, and private efforts to create support for population control policies, and the well-publicized accomplishments of Singapore's family planning program, have heightened awareness of population issues which will aid efforts to lower fertility. The Philippines has embarked on a large-scale family planning program with ambitious targets in terms of fewer births. Other states in the area lag behind, but the levels of concern and of activity are rising generally.

Increased participation in, ownership of, and control over modern economic activities by indigenous populations is a prominent, and at times the leading, economic priority of Southeast Asian states. These states have been aggressive in using the powers of government to transform the alien-dominated economies inherited with independence into national economies which assure that the gains—material and psychic—to be realized from economic expansion accrue predominantly to members of the national society. Foreign investment is closely controlled and regulated. Governments intervene to see that such investment is accompanied by an inflow of foreign exchange and is not funded by local borrowings, that nationals are employed, trained, and upgraded, that profits earned and remitted do not compensate excessively for the foreign entrepreneurship and risk bearing provided, and that ownership is ultimately transferred to nationals. Access to markets and resources is arranged by negotiation, a decision-making process analogous to bilateral monopoly, in which the increasing sophistication and technical expertise of Southeast Asians administering foreign investment policies and the intangible weight of host country sovereignty maintain a preponderance of bargaining power which offers assurance that host country interests will be adequately protected.

The existing situation represents an advanced stage in a prolonged process of bringing the economies of the region under indigenous control in which these states have moved steadily from target to target. There were substantial transfers of alien-owned assets with the transfer of political power after World War II as the Chettyar moneylenders in Burma and major Dutch holdings in Indonesia and French interests in North Vietnam were expropriated. Following independence, the pressures of economic nationalism impinged disproportionately on the Chinese and other Asian aliens whose activities and enterprises involved skills within the capabilities of nationals, and expansion of indigenous participation in retail trade, the importation and distribution of manufactures of consumer goods, and domestic trade in cereals was widespread. As experiences and training of nationals enlarged their capabilities, the pressures of economic nationalism shifted to the larger Western enterprises, and the past decade and a half has witnessed the steady transfer of such enterprises to Southeast Asians. Of equal importance in bringing the economies of the area under indigenous control have been policy structures devised to reserve a preponderant part of economic expansion to nationals. Inasmuch as economic growth in the Philippines, Thailand, Singapore, and Malaysia has been maintained at respectable rates, the relative importance of alien and Western enterprise in these states has contracted steadily with little overt expropriation. Today the focus of economic nationalism in the region has shifted from the threat to the sovereignty of the host country arising in the activities of resident aliens and foreign direct investment enterprises to concern for excessive dependence upon Japan as a source of imports and as a market for exports—a change which has proceeded to the point where resurgence of Japanese hegemony is a perceived threat.

Finally, Southeast Asian leaders are involved in managing the integration of their economies into the international trading and monetary systems. Under World Bank leadership, industrial countries with major interests in Southeast Asia have been organized into country consortia for the Philippines, Thailand, and Indonesia. These industrial countries, together with the World Bank and its subsidiary institutions and the International Monetary Fund and the Asian Development Bank, assure a flow of outside resources critically important to the achievement of development goals of Southeast Asian governments.

The growth since the mid-1960s of the so-called Eurocurrency markets, undisciplined by national policies and regulatory agencies, has resulted in an enormous increase in internationally mobile funds seeking profitable investment.[5] At the same time, economic growth maintained by the open economies in Southeast Asia has improved their credit-worthiness, and the skills of financial policy administrators and private bankers are reflected in financial structures capable of tapping private international capital markets. Private and public borrowing in Eurocurrency markets has become a major source of outside capital available to the open economies of the region.[6] Southeast Asian beneficiaries of this new source of funds—political leaders challenged to maintain the pace of economic expansion and industrialization and private banking and entrepreneurial interests—understand that continued access to Eurocurrency funds requires the balancing of debt service capacity with the volume of new borrowings. This

[5]Estimated foreign currency credits channeled through European banks, the major component of Eurocurrencies, increased from $44 billion in 1969 to $205 billion at the end of 1975. Bank for International Settlements, *Forty-sixth Annual Report* (1975–76), p. 83, and *Forty-fifth Annual Report* (1974–75), p. 141.

[6]During 1974 and 1975, publicized Eurocurrency credits obtained by Indonesia, Malaysia, and the Philippines totaled $3.7 billion. Federal Reserve Bank of San Francisco, *Pacific Basin Economic Indicators,* September 1976, pp. 30, 49, 62.

constraint will ensure support by Southeast Asian states for efforts of the Group of 77 to negotiate arrangements for moratoria on the service of external debt and/or the restructuring and forgiveness of such debt.

If the coming decade sees no substantial escalation in levels of outside support for internal dissidence and rebellion—weapons and supplies, training of guerrillas, maintenance of sanctuaries— and no open warfare, the structure of economic concerns and priorities which have become prominent in Southeast Asia will continue to preempt the attention of the region's political leaders and the resources at their disposal. Under these circumstances, economic expansion in the pattern of that of the past quarter-century will continue, a process which will support modest industrialization and contraction in the shares of aggregate income generated by agriculture and foreign trade activities. Such growth promises no amelioration of the grossly skewed patterns of income distribution prevailing in the area. On the other hand, if past rates of growth in per capita real income are maintained while the pattern of income distribution remains stable, it will mean that the modest economic growth taking place will be widely distributed and will make the contribution to social stability in the future that it has in the recent past. There also is hope that significant declines in fertility will occur in the region.

Progress toward other normative goals which cannot be subsumed under the economic growth likely to take place will lag. Growth, in and of itself, will not slow the rate of urbanization taking place in the region and thereby mitigate the disturbing private and social costs attending this process; or provide employment opportunities outside agriculture which will keep pace with growth in the labor force; or dampen the bias toward scale and the concentration of modern growth in the vicinity of the capital cities; or significantly change processes of resource exploitation which threaten alarming deterioration in the physical environment.

If the next decade and a half sees intensification of instability fueled by internal dissent and/or subversion supported from the outside, members of the societies affected and their leaders will assign priority to the survival of the political and economic systems with which they are familiar. Confronting such a threat will require the sacrifice of some part of the modest increase in material welfare that otherwise will result, and, moreover, in the end such an effort may prove futile. If this should be the case, radical changes in the organization of production and in the process of collective decision making are likely to be imposed on societies which, because they are nationalistic, when faced by the prospect of such changes will react initially to resist them.

THREE

The Potential for Regionalism

THE BASES FOR REGIONALISM

Southeast Asians generally find regionalism an attractive idea, and they are quick to voice the need for more knowledge of their neighbors and understanding of the heritage they share. Moreover, ample scope exists for exploring the potential for regionalism. Diplomatic missions are exchanged, regional institutions for agricultural research, development planning, public administration, higher education, and so forth, have been brought into existence. The most recent of three attempts to form a regional association of states presently performs a narrow range of functions, but its powers and influence can be expanded if the states of the region can agree to do so.

Subsidiary branches and agencies of the United Nations— World Health Organization (WHO), Food and Agriculture Organization (FAO), International Labor Organization (ILO), International Bank for Reconstruction and Development (IBRD), International Monetary Fund (IMF), United Nations Industrial Development Organization (UNIDO), Economic Commission for Asia and the Far East (ECAFE), and the United Nations Conference on Trade and Development (UNCTAD)—bring representatives of the Southeast Asian states together in forums, thereby increasing their understanding of national priorities and shared interests essential to mutual confidence and trust. Other institutions such as the Asian Development Bank and professional organizations within and without the area bring policy makers and scholars together and in the process heighten the awareness of Southeast Asians in the interests and concerns of their neighbors.

In addition, a common image of colonialism provides a base upon which to build regional cooperation as a vehicle for furthering shared interests. Southeast Asians see their nationalist movements as collective efforts to escape constraints attributable to the exploitative nature of colonialism which prevented the realization of individual and collective capacities for economic and social development. Their exclusion from policy formulation in colonial governments was matched by their subordinate status in the racial hierarchy of economic roles which they believe to have resulted from deliberate policies and practices that blocked access by members of indigenous societies to jobs, markets, and financial resources.

The stereotype image of colonial immigration policy explains the resented Asian aliens in their midst. They are there because it was in the interest of Western enterprise to recruit and transport them and to co-opt them into the laissez faire economies installed by the colonial powers where they prospered and served as a useful counterweight to indigenous nationalism. Colonial systems of education proved inadequate because the economic pluralism of colonial societies deprived them of public support and because they were structured to prepare the few trained for positions in colonial bureaucracies.

Southeast Asians believe, moreover, that the colonial development strategy of comparative advantage ensured their international specialization as "hewers of wood and drawers of water" and, by denying protection to domestic manufactures, prevented industrialization and postponed their entry into the mainstream of material progress. Corollary to this policy was the maintenance of exchange reserve currency systems which exposed the colonies to the full fury of unstable demand conditions in international trade.

The subjective image of their colonial experience shared by Southeast Asians is confirmed for them by incongruities they find in their economic and social development. The open economies of the area are market systems functioning without ideological commitment. Southeast Asian societies are seeking industrial development with a weak commitment to efficiency which is subordinated to a dominant drive to ensure that the manufacturing development taking place is brought under indigenous control. Government intervention in market processes is the rule rather than the exception. Interest rates reflect political criteria, and flows of savings, credit, and capital resources are distorted as a result. Price controls are endemic but are uniformly ineffective in the absence of rationing. Entry to markets and access to resources are tightly controlled, and maximum discretionary authority is reserved to administrators of major economic policies.

Despite the cohesiveness of nationalist movements, today we find the articulation of social and economic classes little changed from colonialism. The ruling elites are isolated from the population generally, and the antithesis of the dominant national capital and the country, of city and village, continues as before. Extreme centralization of government is rationalized in familiar terms: "The peasant requires further tutelage before he can participate in his governance." "Local governments cannot be entrusted with tax bases or to carry out economic functions."

Southeast Asians believe that the pattern of specialization and trade common to their countries was central to the process of colonial exploitation. Such specialization, moreover, is believed to carry risks of price instability, secular deterioration in the terms of trade, the vulnerability of specialized resources to the development of substitutes, and the strategic vulnerability of economies dependent upon the outside world for industrial products including weapons. Primary product specialization is discredited in the minds of Southeast Asians, but the exports of the area remain highly dependent upon a few commodities and a limited number of major markets.

OBSTACLES TO REGIONALISM

Searching for bases for expanded regionalism in Southeast Asia beyond the minds of Southeast Asians is not a fruitful task. The image of colonialism shared by Southeast Asians generally was instrumental to bringing about the demise of colonial rule, but there is scant evidence that it can cause regionalism to flourish. Independence movements are also nationalist movements of societies cemented by a common will to self-governance and confident that achievement of this goal will release latent and powerful capacities for progress. At the core of a nationalist movement is a society comprising those who share essential qualifications for membership which is striving for homogeneity, separateness, and distinctiveness. Such societies are poor building blocks with which to erect a structure of supranational regionalism.

The burden of Southeast Asian history—the divisions among its peoples—is a formidable obstacle to regionalism. The area has been much fought over, and migrations of populations have dispossessed and in some cases decimated other populations. Impressive monuments—Angkor, Ayutthaya, Pagan, Borobadur—confirm that civilizations flourished, expanded, encountered reverses, and were displaced or extinguished. In mainland Southeast Asia, which escaped colonization by the West until the nineteenth century, the enmity of the Burmese and the Thais is a recent and strong memory. Similarly, the traditional animosities between Thais and Khmers, Khmers and Vietnamese, and Thais and Vietnamese, which were renewed by the French in extending and maintaining their rule in the Indochinese peninsula, remain close to the surface. Spain in extending its rule encountered little resistance in converting the peoples in the north of the Philippine archipelago, but Islam, which had captured the minds of Filipinos in the Sulu Archipelago and southwestern Mindanao, proved impenetrable to Spanish proselytizing. The intermittent warfare and piratical raiding of the succeeding centuries fueled a lasting animosity between the Christian north and the Muslim south which is blazing today.

The island empires based upon the commercial importance of the Straits of Malacca which exercised power before the coming of the Europeans left a residue of memories that maintain latent anxieties. This legacy was confirmed during the period of *Konfrontasi* in the 1960s when the racially balanced population of the Malay peninsula reacted instinctively when an Indonesian initiative revived fear of the domination of the Straits of Malacca area by a new island empire. Similarly, the assertion of the Philippine claim to Sabah stirred memories of historical relations between ethnic communities of the Islamic sultanates in the area of the Sulu Archipelago and acerbated tensions between Christian and Muslim peoples in the wider region. Peripheral to the warfare in Indochina were small-scale vendettas between Khmer and Vietnamese and between Lao/Thai and Vietnamese which have roots extending through the history of the area.

Regionalism is also constrained by a legacy of more recent history, the pall of uncertainty obscuring intraregional relations. The states of the area, with the exception of Thailand, have enjoyed relatively brief periods of independent existence. They are concerned for their autonomy and territorial integrity and, given the postindependence history of the area, for good reason. The uncertainties and perceived threats which are a legacy of the prolonged warfare in Vietnam, on balance, seem likely to inhibit rather than encourage joint action by the states of the area over the next decade and a half.

The impact of recent history on Southeast Asian regionalism was brought into sharp focus by the summit conference of Association of Southeast Asian Nations (ASEAN) heads of state which met in Bali in February 1976. The principal accomplishment of the summit, the Treaty of Amity, is a wide-ranging compilation of actions to make Southeast Asia over into a "zone of peace, freedom, and neutrality." Despite the avowed intentions of the ASEAN leaders, specific proposals for cooperation received rough handling. Indonesian enthusiasm, backed by the Philippines, for some kind of joint ASEAN approach to defense was squelched by the indifference of Malaysia and Thailand, who feel most immediately threatened with externally supported subversion and intensified insurgency. Singapore's proposal of the formation of an ASEAN free-trade area in conjunction with the initiation of the planning of joint industrial establishments to serve the region foundered on Indonesian opposition which undoubtedly was welcome to the Malaysian leadership. The Philippines urged that the Treaty of Amity include automatic mediation or arbitration mechanisms for the settlement of disputes among the

ASEAN states, but this expired promptly in the face of Malaysian fear that behind the Philippine proposal was a plan to revive that country's claim to Sabah.

The Treaty of Amity also included an invitation to other Southeast Asian states to subscribe to the agreement. Hanoi responded icily, attacking ASEAN in the North Vietnamese Army daily newspaper, *Quan Doi Nhan Dan,* as an American vehicle for rallying reactionary forces to oppose revolutionary movements in Southeast Asia. Hanoi singled out Indonesia as the "regional policeman of the U.S." and accused Indonesia of "openly committing an armed invasion of East Timor."

Another major obstacle to regionalism within Southeast Asia is the colonial legacy of political and economic isolation of state from state. The industrial revolution in northwestern Europe was followed by a far-reaching change in colonial policy as mercantilism succumbed to laissez faire capitalism and comparative advantage. These policies, in conjunction with direct rule, hastened the development of the colonies as markets for the manufactures of the industrial West and as sources of supply of tropical foodstuffs and industrial raw materials. Although the "open door" was extended to colonial trade policy by the British and the Dutch, the political and investment relationships between these countries and their colonies ensured that the trade of a colony would be concentrated in exchanges with the colonial power. The latecomers to the race for colonies—France and the United States—were more aggressive in monopolizing the trade of their colonies by mutual trade preferences. The modest economic development taking place in the region, therefore, became a process in which the colonies "faced outward, turning their backs to their neighbors." As a result, colonial development produced little regional specialization and integration, and this pattern has persisted to the present.

Partial exceptions to this generalization were Burma, which specialized in the production of rice for markets in India and other British colonies around the Bay of Bengal; Thailand, whose exports were concentrated in rice shipments to food deficit areas around the South China Sea; and Singapore, which flourished as a transit port through which the raw materials of the region moved westward in exchange for a return flow of manufactures funneled to markets adjacent to the Malacca Straits and the South China Sea.

The structure of manufacturing output in Southeast Asia which reflects the industrial development strategy common to the countries of the region also contributes to the pattern of economic isolation of state from state. Newly independent governments were faced by the necessity to make good the promises of successful nationalist movements. One such promise was the transformation of the colonial-type economies by industrial development, and each country initially sought to hasten this process by recourse to directly productive public enterprise. The results of this industrialization policy proved uniformly disappointing, however, and over time the states of the area turned to "import substitution" as a vehicle for accelerating manufacturing development based upon private enterprise and the internal market. Such a strategy typically was implemented by a combination of high levels of protection maintained by tariffs and currency overvaluation, subsidization of manufacturing activities by allocations of foreign exchange and credit and remission of tariffs and internal taxes, and limitation of competitive pressures by strict control over access to markets and resources. While the experience with industrial efforts has varied widely over the area, manufacturing output has increased generally. Although the inadequacies of import substitution led to its abandonment in the extreme form dependent upon currency overvaluation, modest expansion in manufacturing sustained, for the most part, by high levels of protection, has continued in Southeast Asia.

Because industrial development is dependent upon protection, manufacturing output has tended to reflect historical patterns of imports of manufactures which were relatively uniform from country to country. As a result, output is concentrated in consumer goods and relatively simple industrial products— processed foods, clothing, footwear, textiles, petroleum refining, rubber manufactures, simple metal fabrication, automobile assembly, pharmaceuticals, simple industrial chemicals, and miscellaneous manufactures—a pattern which varies little from state to state.[7] The essence of regional economic integration is the "division of labor" or specialization within the region, but manufacturing development in Southeast Asia has resulted not in economic integration, but the opposite. National manufacturing interests, heavily subsidized, sheltered from competition, and reinforced by the longings of Southeast Asians generally for industrialization, will resist progress toward effective economic regionalism over the next decade.[8]

REGIONALISM—RHETORIC AND REALITY

In the early postwar years, Southeast Asian governments were undeviating in their support of the United Nations, which they visualized as a forum where international public opinion could be mobilized to eliminate the last vestiges of colonialism. Regional unity within the United Nations also was sustained by a shared perception of the role of that institution in enlarging the sovereignty of small states through a viable system of collective security. Although the faith of Southeast Asian societies in collective security was shaken by the collapse of Nationalist resistance in China and the subsequent war in Korea, it was still strong enough to ensure regional unity in the Bandung Conference of 1955. With important leadership from Indonesia's Sukarno and Burma's U Nu, this meeting of leaders of less developed countries took the first important step in organizing these states into a viable bloc which has maintained impressive unity and gained influence in the turbulent years since its founding. Cold war

[7]In this type of industrialization, additional industries tend to materialize in a sequence determined by the bill of imports and the growth in the indigenous capacity to invest in manufacturing enterprises. The economies of Southeast Asia vary considerably in the level of development achieved, but insofar as they are at a roughly comparable stage of development, the structure of manufacturing output will be similar from country to country.

[8]Other aspects of postindependence development in the area carry the same message. The various states have brought into existence national merchant marines, national airlines, and national capital markets which, over the foreseeable future, will inhibit regional integration.

tensions in the area of eastern Asia, which culminated in the prolonged Vietnam War, as well as concern for the hegemonial ambitions of Sukarno's Indonesia, subsequently eroded the regional unity of purpose evident in the common opposition to colonialism and cooperative efforts to enlarge the neutralism of the area.

Within this overall pattern of change, efforts to explore the potential for Southeast Asian regionalism have persisted and interaction between Southeast Asians in positions of leadership has expanded steadily. A number of initiatives have involved cooperation with states in Asia beyond Southeast Asia and with countries in the wider world. This was the case of the Colombo Plan, which was brought into existence with British Empire leadership, the Economic Commission for Asia and the Far East (ECAFE) and its successor, the Economic and Social Commission for Asia and the Pacific (ESCAP), regional organizations of the United Nations, the Simla Conference of 1955,[9] which resulted from Indian leadership, and the Southeast Asia Treaty Organization, a creature of the United States. Among other groupings centering on Southeast Asia, but including countries beyond the area, are the Lower Mekong Basin Coordinating Committee, the Asian Development Bank (ADB), and the Asia and Pacific Council.

Coordinate with Southeast Asian participation in wider groupings have been the successive attempts to establish an inclusive intraregional organization. The initial attempt was the Association of Southeast Asia (ASA), which was founded in 1961 by the Philippines, Thailand, and Malaya, with other countries sending observers to the founding conference. Activities of ASA were interrupted in 1963 when the Philippines advanced its claim to North Borneo (Sabah) and diplomatic relations between the

[9]The Simla Conference of representatives of 13 South and Southeast Asian states was convened to discuss the formation of a regional organization similar to the Organization for European Economic Cooperation to coordinate the use of United States aid funds available for Asian development. The conference, which broke up on May 13, 1955, after five days of meetings, issued a terse communiqué stating that "there would be no advantage in establishing such an organization."

Philippines and Malaysia were suspended.[10] Although diplomatic relations between the two countries were resumed in 1965, ASA did not flourish thereafter. During its brief existence, ASA held ad hoc consultations on regional issues and maintained joint committees and working parties.[11] In 1967, ASEAN was formed by the ASA states plus Indonesia and Singapore. ASEAN has remained active and has acquired stature as a forum for consultation among the participating states.

Despite this record, the accomplishments of the purely regional Southeast Asian organizations have been modest. Regional projects such as the Asian Highway and the Mekong River Project have been discussed and tentative national responsibilities and commitments planned. With the support of outside funding, studies have been made of the impact of development of the water resources of the Mekong River basin. Regional projects have also been studied and discussed under the auspices of broader regional organizations such as ECAFE and ADB. For example, studies have been made of the practices of international shipping conferences in setting freight rates and penalty rates imposed for shipments to ports charged with inefficient cargo handling. The benefits and costs of a regional merchant marine which would provide services presently controlled by conferences of major ocean shipping lines have been analyzed. A similar enterprise was the joint study of the feasibility of a regional international airline. In addition, extraregional and regional organizations have commissioned studies and working papers dealing with the benefits of a regional customs union and the implementation of such a scheme, but no substantive progress has proved possible. Similarly, the gains to be realized from harmonization of national development plans to prevent the waste and inefficiency arising in

[10]The political union of Malaya, Singapore, and the British colonies of North Borneo and Sarawak into Malaysia took place in 1962. Singapore was subsequently expelled from Malaysia in 1965.

[11]"Maphilindo," a regional grouping involving Malaysia, the Philippines, and Indonesia, was proclaimed at a summit meeting of the heads of these states at the height of the tension over the formation of Malaysia. The decision of Indonesia to initiate the stage of *Konfrontasi* involving hostilities between Malaysian and British forces and irregular forces supported by Indonesia brought an end to Maphilindo, which never amounted to more than a slogan or sentiment.

duplication of productive capacity within the region have received attention.

The modest accomplishments from efforts to expand regional cooperation reflect the limited economic integration within the area. Intraregional trade accounts for a relatively small fraction of the total trade of the states of the area, and this ratio is changing slowly. For the three years 1970 through 1972, intraregional exports of the 10 Southeast Asian countries for which data are available averaged 1,681 million dollars annually and accounted for 23.5 percent of the global exports of these countries (see Table 1). The proportion of intraregional exports in total exports varied from a high of 83 percent in the case of Laos, which accounted for less than 1 percent of the exports of the area, to a low of 2 percent in the case of the Philippines. Malaysia and Singapore, which dominated intraregional trade, together accounted for 48 percent of the global exports of the region and just over two-thirds of intraregional exports. Moreover, trade between Malaysia and Singapore averaged $765 million annually or 45 percent of intraregional exports. In contrast, Indonesia, the Philippines, and Thailand, which accounted for 46 percent of global exports of the region, provided only one-quarter of intraregional exports.

The modest level of economic integration in Southeast Asia indicated by the pattern of intraregional exports must be scaled down substantially when account is taken of the volume of exports that are transshipped through Singapore with only marginal value added by processing or packaging. Thanks to its strategic location and natural harbor, Singapore developed as an *entrepôt,* assembling the produce of the region for shipment to the West and distributing the manufactures received in return. Recent years have seen persistent efforts on the part of other Southeast Asian states to develop port facilities and to expand direct trade with nonregional markets, but the natural advantages and the efficient services maintained at Singapore have ensured continuation of that port's traditional role.

For the three years 1970–1972, export shipments from Singapore of foods and raw materials produced in Southeast Asia averaged some $625 million, including shipments of natural rubber valued at $332 million and of petroleum and products of some

TABLE 1
Intraregional Export Trade in Southeast Asia, 1970–1972
(annual average $U.S. millions)

Exporting Country	Country of Destination										Total Intra-regional Exports	Global Exports	Ratio of Intra-regional to Global Exports (percent)
	Brunei	Burma	Cam-bodia	Indo-nesia	Laos	Malay-sia	Philip-pines	Singa-pore	Thai-land	South Viet-nam			
Brunei*	—	1.5	—	0.1	—	62.2	4.3	8.1	5.1	—	81.3	141.2	57.6
Burma	—	—	—	3.5	—	4.1	2.7	10.1	—	—	20.4	118.3	17.2
Cambodia	—	—	—	—	—	—	—	1.1	0.1	1.3	2.5	16.0	15.6
Indonesia	—	0.2	—	—	—	49.5	19.8	149.4	0.3	0.2	219.4	1,344.1	16.3
Laos	—	—	—	—	—	2.4	—	0.2	1.9	—	4.5	5.4	83.3
Malaysia	9.0	3.9	—	10.8	—	—	29.4	367.1	17.4	1.4	439.0	1,663.0	26.4
Philippines	0.6	—	—	2.9	—	1.0	—	10.3	3.1	3.6	21.5	1,093.9	2.0
Singapore	34.1	4.7	9.5	74.7†	—	398.0	10.1	—	59.8	115.4	706.3	1,804.4	39.1
Thailand	—	—	5.7	21.1	22.1	43.0	16.3	67.0	—	10.6	185.8	874.1	21.3
South Vietnam	—	—	—	—	—	—	—	0.4	—	—	0.4	7.9	5.1
Total	43.7	10.3	15.2	113.1	22.1	560.2	82.6	613.7	87.7	132.5	1,681.1	7,168.3	23.5

*Average for 1971–1972.
†Imports from Singapore reported by Indonesia.
NOTE: A dash signifies either that no exports were recorded or that the recorded value of exports was less than $50,000.
SOURCE: United Nations, Yearbook of International Trade Statistics, 1974.

$120 million (see Table 2). In view of Singapore's small area and extensive industrial development and urbanization, internal production could not have accounted for significant exports of these products, although substantial value was added by refining of imported petroleum and minor increments in value resulted from the processing, grading, and packaging of primary products shipped through Singapore. It is not possible to determine the proportion of the raw materials exported by other regional states which Singapore retained, but, except in the case of petroleum, this ratio was not high for the commodities listed. When the value of Singapore's exports of the produce of Southeast Asia during 1970–1972 is compared to the value of intraregional exports of $1.7 billion, it seems reasonably clear that intraregional exports retained within the area may have accounted for no more than one-sixth of the global exports of the Southeast Asian states.

In assessing the economic integration within the region, it is also necessary to take into consideration the very high proportion of foods and raw materials in intraregional exports. During the period 1963–1965, intraregional exports of foods and raw materials of the eight countries for which data are available totaled $698 million, or two-thirds of the intraregional exports of the area for that period (see Table 3).[12] If it were possible to adjust the exports of Singapore (which accounted for almost one-half of intraregional exports of the eight countries tabulated) to eliminate the transshipment through Singapore of manufactures from the outside world, the proportion of retained intraregional exports other than foods and raw materials would be a minor fraction of intraregional exports.

Meaningful economic integration requires a specialization within the region which spreads across the spectrum of goods traded from foods and raw materials through capital equipment and high-technology manufactures. Southeast Asia has yet to progress beyond a preliminary stage of economic regionalism.

[12]The inclusion of Indonesia and Burma, the two states missing from the tabulation in Table 3, would raise this ratio somewhat, as the exports of these countries are highly concentrated in foods and raw materials. Comparably *complete* data for more recent years is not available, but the limited annual data that are available support the conclusions presented here.

TABLE 2
Transit Trade of Singapore in Foods and Raw Materials
Produced in Southeast Asia, 1970–1972
(exports f.o.b., annual average $U.S. millions)

	Trade of Singapore	
	Imports of Foods and Raw Materials from Southeast Asia	*Exports of Foods and Raw Materials*
Coffee, tea, cacao, spices (07)*		68.3
Coffee (071)	22.6	
Spices (075)	41.8	
Total	64.4	
Crude materials, excluding fuels (2)		420.6
Natural rubber (2311)	332.4	
Wood, lumber cork (24)	38.1	
Total	370.5	
Mineral fuels (3)		80.0‡
Petroleum and products	120.0†	
Animal and vegetable oils and fats (4)		55.8
Palm oil	37.1	
Coconut oil	10.6	
Total	47.7	
Total of above categories	602.6	624.7

*Standard International Trade Classification categories in parentheses.

†Estimated value of exports of petroleum to Singapore from Brunei, Sarawak, and Indonesia. The principal part of Singapore's petroleum imports during 1970–1972 came from Middle Eastern countries.

‡Prorated share of Southeast Asian supplies in total exports of petroleum products from Singapore.

SOURCE: United Nations, *Yearbook of International Trade Statistics, 1973, 1974.*

TABLE 3
Intraregional Exports of Raw Materials and Foodstuffs in Southeast Asia, 1963–1965
(annual average $U.S. millions, percent of intraregional exports)

	Live Animals and Food (0)	Beverages and Tobacco (1)	Crude Materials, Inedible (2)	Mineral Fuels, etc. (3)	Animal and Vegetable Oils (4)	Intra-regional Exports of Raw Materials (1–4)	Total Intra-regional Exports	Ratio Exports of Raw Materials to Intra-regional Exports (percent)
Brunei	—	—	0.6	59.6	—	60.2	60.4	99.7
Cambodia	13.4	—	3.3	0.1	—	16.8	18.0	93.3
Laos	0.1	—	0.7	—	—	0.8	0.7	100.0
Malaysia*	41.1	4.1	134.4	40.6	12.0	232.2	284.6	81.6
Singapore	93.7	14.5	20.3	78.6	3.5	210.6	497.5	42.4
Philippines	0.3	0.1	0.4	0.4	—	1.2	2.3	52.2
Thailand	128.3	0.3	43.8	0.7	0.1	173.1	175.5	98.6
South Vietnam	1.5	0.2	0.7	—	0.2	2.6	9.9	26.3
Total	278.3	19.2	204.2	180.0	15.8	697.5	1,048.9	66.5

*Reported exports of Malaya, Sabah, and Sarawak, less mutual trade.
SOURCE: UN Economic Commission for Asia and the Far East, *Foreign Trade Statistics of Asia and the Far East, 1963, 1964, 1965*. Exports classified in Standard International Trade Classification in one-digit categories as indicated.

FOUR

Southeast Asia in the Group of 77

The package of Southern "demands" that emerged in the Declaration on the Establishment of a New International Economic Order approved by the Sixth Special Session of the UN General Assembly in the spring of 1974, in the Charter of Economic Rights and Duties of States approved by the General Assembly in December 1974, and in the Lima Declaration of the Second General Conference of the UN Industrial Development Organization of March 1975, received the unanimous approval of the participating less developed countries (LDCs), and very few negative votes were registered by participating industrial countries.

In the area of commodity trade, the South seeks higher prices and expanded proceeds from the range of major primary commodity exports of the LDCs. In the absence of fortuitous and unlikely changes in demand conditions for these commodities, achievement of these goals will require substantial Northern funding of buffer stocks or compensating income transfers to the commodity-producing countries. In connection with unrequited aid transfers, the South demands that developed countries meet aid targets to which they subscribed in the UN's International Development Strategy for the Second UN Development Decade, that they increase their contributions to the emergency fund created under UN auspices in response to the fuel and the food crises of 1973–1974, and that the North be prepared to renegotiate the debt obligations of LDCs experiencing difficulties in meeting debt service payments. Presumably, such negotiations are expected to result in substantial write-offs of these obligations.[13]

Insofar as foreign investment is concerned, the South demands greater access to international capital markets and the elimination of traditional legal restraints on the expropriation of direct investment. To deal with multinational corporations, the South proposes that developing countries participate in policing the practices of the corporations of their nationals to ensure that the benefits accruing to the host country from the overseas activities of multinational corporations are increased.

In the field of technology transfer, the LDCs want the industrial countries (1) to provide funds for the creation, expansion, and modernization of scientific and technological institutions to enhance the capabilities of the South for adaptive research, (2) to "persuade" multinational corporations to adapt the technological aspects of their overseas activities to host country development needs, and (3) to support changes in patent laws and other measures which will facilitate and lower the costs of technology transfers to the less developed world.

The LDCs also demand a greater voice in the management of the international monetary system and reform of the system to provide an international reserve-creating process which will enlarge the share of the South in the distribution of the additional reserves created.

The voice of Southeast Asia in the concert of Southern voices will be relatively weak because regionalism within the area is little developed. The stridency with which this region confronts the North will also be modulated by the Southeast Asian experience with independence. Southeast Asians generally have not been disabused of their nationalist idealism; they still believe that there is a reservoir of will and capabilities within their societies which will sustain economic and social progress. The extreme disillusionment and the anthropomorphological response which dominates social criticism in Latin America appears to be a function of

[13]This assessment was confirmed by the agreement reached by the Group of 77 countries in their meeting in Manila in early February 1976 to thresh out a Southern "plan" to be presented at the subsequent UNCTAD conference held in Nairobi in May 1976.

the prolonged period of nominal independence of those states. Latin American societies threw out their colonial rulers in the first quarter of the nineteenth century, but after 150 years of formal sovereignty, the "good life" has not materialized for Latin Americans generally. This experience has led Latin Americans to believe that international specialization, capitalism, and foreign investment prevent social progress in the area and must be radically reformed or, better still, replaced by another international economic order. In Southeast Asia, on the other hand, the experiences of the two decades or so they have been independent have not caused these societies to reject the normative expectations promised by their successful nationalist movements.

Another aspect of the social environment in Southeast Asia which contrasts sharply with that in Latin America is a consequence of the indifference of the West to the opportunities to colonize Southeast Asia. Colonial powers organized and ruled colonies in the region, but they did not people them. For the most part, the members of Western societies who lived and worked in Southeast Asia remained transient residents. As a result, with the exception of the Philippines, the collapse of colonialism in Southeast Asia was not followed by the transfer of power to alien or alien-dominated mestizo elites as occurred in Latin America. Eurasians in Southeast Asia have not inherited power—they are few in number and are economically and politically impotent. The phenomenon of "internal colonialism" as a distinctively racial phenomenon and as it is identified by scholars of Latin America is embryonic in Southeast Asia and is likely to remain so for some time to come.

Southeast Asia and Latin America also differ radically in patterns of land ownership. With the exception of the Philippines, land ownership in Southeast Asia is widely distributed and the number of landless laborers in the various states of the area is small relative to the number of small holders and tenants.[14] Pres-

---

[14]In the absence of treasure to loot and mineral wealth to be extracted by enslaved labor, the Philippines remained a remote backwater administered by the missionary religious orders with the secular Spanish population concentrated in Manila and supported by the "galleon trade" with Mexico. Agricultural development was left to the Filipinos and to the land-based mestizo

123

sure of population on land resources is an ominous cloud obscuring Southeast Asia's future, but the potential fruitfulness of agricultural resources and widespread distribution of land promise to sustain the modest expectations of the peasant populations of the region through the next decade.[15]

Participation of Southeast Asian states in the Group of 77 will also be influenced by the perceptions of these regimes of the threat of "neocolonialism" and "economic imperialism." These societies have been reassured by the withdrawal of the sovereignty of the colonial powers—France, the Netherlands, Great Britain, and the United States—a withdrawal accomplished over a relatively brief period except in Indochina, which remained a cold war battleground for three decades. The "colonial drain," the massive export surplus which characterized the trade of the states of the area in the latter decades of colonial rule, has been replaced by a substantial import surplus as external claims on output—interest charges on external debt, the earnings of direct foreign investment, pension obligations to foreigners, budgetary subventions, and so forth—were drastically scaled down or repudiated.[16] Expropriation of assets owned by Asian aliens resident in the region have been extensive, transfers of foreign-owned enterprises to Southeast Asians have proceeded steadily, and entry of new foreign capital is subject to strict control and continued surveillance. These circumstances have reassured Southeast Asian leaders dealing with foreign investors

---

"caciques" (Filipino/Chinese and Filipino/Spanish) who steadily increased their holdings of land and regional political power once the islands were opened to trade and economic development following the Napoleonic wars.

[15]Java is a glaring exception to this generalization, not because concentration of land ownership is prominent but because of the sheer pressure of population on the fertile land resources of that island.

[16]Conversion of the "colonial drain" into a substantial import surplus is a mixed blessing for LDCs as an import surplus measures the compensating finance in the form of foreign private and official investment, economic aid, and balance-of-payments assistance, which must materialize to make the import surplus possible. It is also the measure of the increasing dependency of the country experiencing such a surplus on the outside world.

and their enterprises that the sovereignty of the state they represent is essentially intact.

The voice of Southeast Asia will also reflect the interest of the societies in the region and their leaders in the various demands making up the Southern bill of development rights. These societies will recognize an important stake in participation by their governments in reform of the international monetary system because changes in this area promise to increase substantially the flow of resources from the North to the South. For the same reason, the states of Southeast Asia will fall in line behind the Southern demand that developed countries meet aid targets to which they have subscribed in international forums.

On the other hand, the interest of Southeast Asian societies in international collaboration on commodity problems will vary widely among states and with respect to particular commodities and, on balance, will moderate the voice of Southeast Asia as compared to other regions of the less developed world. The major commodity exports of Southeast Asia are rice, sugar, coconut products, palm oil, forest products, rubber, tin, copper, and petroleum. With the exception of rice and sugar, these commodities are not afforded substantial protection by price policies in importing countries. Moreover, in general, and in contrast to such internationally traded commodities as tobacco, coffee, tea, and cacao, they do not serve as important bases for excise taxation in importing countries which raises the internal prices of these commodities and restricts their consumption.[17] Finally, the value added to these commodities by processing where shipment may take place either in unprocessed or processed form is not a major economic consideration. All rice moving in international trade is milled, and sugar moves as centrifugal sugar requiring only minor additional refining. Palm oil must be pressed from the kernels before shipping, and expressing the oil from copra is a simple process which provides little employment and adds little value. Most of the tin and copper are shipped from the producing countries as concentrates, and refining does not offer substantial benefits either in terms of value added or employment.

[17]Petroleum products are an exception to this generalization.

Forest products and petroleum are major exceptions to the foregoing generalization. The processing of logs and timber into lumber, plywood, and other forestry products, in general, is subject to relatively high levels of effective protection in industrial countries, which inhibits the development of processing industries in Southeast Asia. In the case of petroleum, economies of scale in the transport of crude oil and protectionist policies in consuming countries have led to dispersal of refining facilities to developed and less developed countries alike. Member countries of the OPEC cartel are moving to expand refining facilities and to develop petrochemical and fertilizer industries, which suggests that the interest of the petroleum-producing states in the region (Indonesia, Malaysia [Sarawak], and Brunei) in the value added from the processing of petroleum can be adequately protected by participating in OPEC.

The Southeast Asian states probably recognize a modest interest in the potential scarcity premium to be obtained by restricting commodity exports. In some cases, vegetable oils and nonferrous metals, for example, the possibilities of substitution of other commodities in production damp inelasticity expectations. All commodities face the threat of substitutes in one form or another. Tin is at present an exception to this generalization, and the International Tin Study Group has acquired experience and confidence in exploring the monopoly potential of producing interests in the international tin market.

The regional interest in international commodity collaboration also will be influenced by existing bilateral relationships between Southeast Asian states and major industrial countries. An obvious case is the Philippines' interest in its traditional quota in the United States sugar market. This interest is in jeopardy at present, as Congress did not renew the system of marketing quotas used to maintain high levels of protection for the inefficient American beet sugar industry when the Sugar Act of 1968 expired in 1973. As sugar prices continue to recede from the unprecedented levels of 1973–74, pressures to reestablish the quota system will increase. If this occurs, we can expect the Philippine interest in preferential access to the United States sugar market to moderate its enthusiasm for submerging its commodity interests

126

with those of the LDCs generally. Less strong but probably a moderating factor of some significance is the residual bilateralism in the trade and financial relationships of Malaysia with the British Commonwealth. The rapid integration of the Southeast Asian states with the dynamic Japanese economy over the past decade and a half has created a regional interest which Southeast Asian states also may be reluctant to pool with those of the LDCs generally. Confronted by a climate of virulent economic nationalism and suspicion of Japan inherited from World War II, the Japanese have been imaginative in using supplier credits to expand the capacity of the area to produce material inputs required by Japan's economy and in accepting repayment of such credits in shipments of the materials produced.

The foregoing is only a partial assessment of the Southeast Asian interest in international commodity collaboration. It is focused on collaboration in the traditional sense of efforts to maximize proceeds from marketings of commodities for which global demand is believed to be inelastic. The interest of Southeast Asian states in this type of collaboration is, as suggested, likely to remain limited. The Southeast Asian states can be expected, however, to maintain a strong interest in high and stable prices for primary commodities supported by buffer stocks and/or compensatory financing of shortfalls in foreign exchange earnings funded by outside contributions.

The interest of the Southeast Asian states in nonreciprocal tariff preferences for manufactures is not a strong one. Manufacturing development in the area, with the important exception of Singapore, is based upon the internal market and is highly protected. The share of value added by manufacturing in the export earnings of Southeast Asian states is relatively minor and is dominated by the processing of major commodity exports—the refining of sugar and petroleum and the processing of logs and timber into lumber, plywood, and other products. Although manufacturing development in the area is highly protected, these states do have the capability to compete in industrial country markets with a range of light manufactures—clothing, footwear, electronics assembly, and so forth—if nonreciprocal tariff preferences should exempt their exports from tariff duties which presently protect the producers of these commodities in developed countries. If nonreciprocal tariff preferences are generalized and global, the perceived interest of the Southeast Asian states in such preferences, with the exception of Singapore, is likely to remain a minor one. They will not be optimistic in assessing their competitiveness vis-à-vis such countries as South Korea, Taiwan, Hong Kong, and Singapore in the area of eastern Asia, and India and Mediterranean basin countries as well.[18]

The economic leaders of Southeast Asian states are aware that levels of industrial protection in industrial states have been reduced substantially in bilateral and multilateral negotiations over the past four decades. This is not to say that a relatively low ratio of duties collected to the value of dutiable imports does not conceal levels of protection that exclude imports and shelter inefficiency, but to suggest that the stake perceived by Southeast Asian leaders in generalized global preferences will be a relatively modest one. This will be the case if these states decide that only a small proportion of the trade in manufactures they are capable of producing and exporting can be diverted to their producers by the elimination of present tariff barriers.

The remaining Southern demands are unlikely to sustain deep interest in Southeast Asian societies and their leaders. The states of the region will endorse these demands, however, because they will be perceived as useful bargaining counters which may add marginally to Southern leverage in negotiations with the North.

Despite such obvious inconsistencies in the Southern bill of development rights as the conflict between the demand that the North acknowledge the host country's untrammeled right to expropriate foreign investment and the proposal that Southern access to international capital markets be enlarged, it would be presumptuous to label the Southeast Asian "voice" supporting Southern demands as rhetorical. The process of drawing up a list of demands is viewed as a rational step in establishing a Southern

[18]Singapore, with per capita income approaching $600, will not be optimistic in assessing its chances of capturing and retaining a substantial share of markets opened to LDCs by nonreciprocal preferences. To do so would expose Singapore to discriminatory action within the Group of 77.

bargaining position preliminary to meaningful negotiations between the LDCs and the developed countries. The states of Southeast Asia may be unrealistic in assessing the bargaining clout of the Southern bloc, but they are quite realistic in assuming that meaningful negotiations are going to take place.

The participation of the states of Southeast Asia in the Group of 77 will reflect their assessment of the magnitude and distribution of the gains likely to result from the Southern demands. It is unlikely that those in power in Southeast Asia expect the gains from concerted action by the Group of 77 to increase substantially the total financial resources available to their countries in the near future. Nor are they likely to expect that the redistribution of the financial resources transferred from North to South will favor Southeast Asia disproportionately. On the other hand, these leaders will recognize that important precedents are at stake in negotiations over Southern demands.

The states of Southeast Asia will support the bill of Southern demands and they will do so for largely the same reasons: peer group pressure, the need perceived by the leaders of the area to tend their images as nationalists, and because they see their participation in the Southern bloc as carrying little risk of loss and the possibility of significant gains as the new international trading and monetary systems evolve. As nationals of small states, Southeast Asians derive self-esteem and psychic benefits from the role played by their leaders in international forums. Moreover, with the exception of Burma and the Indochinese states, Southeast Asians and their leaders probably attribute incremental security to international collaboration based upon common interests. Safety is not assured by numbers, but they perceive marginal gains stemming from the capability of the concert of LDCs to mobilize public opinion in world forums.

Selected Bibliography

Asian Development Bank: *Southeast Asia's Economy in the 1970s,* Praeger Publishers, Inc., New York, 1971. A team of specialists led by Professor Hla Myint surveys the status and future prospects of agricultural development, industrialization, external economic relations, foreign investment, human fertility, and peace in Southeast Asia at the close of the UN's Development Decade of the 1960s. The optimism shared generally by the contributors serves to emphasize the importance of such recent economic changes as the international monetary crises of 1971 and 1973 and the formation of the OPEC cartel.

Boeke, Julius H.: *Economics and Economic Policy of Dual Societies,* H. D. Tjeenk Willink and Zoon, Haarlem, 1953. Boeke's concept of sociological dualism provided a rationale for Dutch colonial policy in Indonesia and initiated prolonged controversy which clarified the various aspects of dualism in development.

Furnivall, J. S.: *Colonial Policy and Practice,* Cambridge University Press, Cambridge, 1948. Summarizes the major contributions to our knowledge of colonialism of an English economist and colonial civil servant long resident in Southeast Asia. Furnivall's concepts and generalizations have most direct application to Burma.

Geertz, Clifford: *Agricultural Involution: The Process of Ecological Change in Indonesia,* University of California Press, Berkeley, 1963. Geertz's analysis of the processes of rural change in Indonesia illuminates the uniqueness of Java in the diversity of Southeast Asia. Useful counterweight to and extension of Boeke's analysis of Javanese culture.

Golay, Frank H.: *The Philippines: Public Policy and National Economic Development,* Cornell University Press, Ithaca, N.Y., 1961. The author seeks

131

to understand the goals, the development strategy, and the consequences of Philippine economic policies from 1946 to 1960, the first decade and a half of Philippine independence.

Golay, Frank H., Ralph Anspach, M. Ruth Pfanner, and Eliezer B. Ayal: *Underdevelopment and Economic Nationalism in Southeast Asia,* Cornell University Press, Ithaca, N.Y., 1969. Four economists specializing on Southeast Asia analyze the efforts of the Burmese, Thai, Indonesian, Philippine, South Vietnamese, and Cambodian societies to ensure that the benefits of economic development accrue preponderantly to nationals of the country concerned.

Hall, D. G. E.: *A History of Southeast Asia,* 3d ed., Macmillan & Co., Ltd., London, 1968. The standard history of the political entities and peoples of Southeast Asia. Particularly valuable for an understanding of the pre-European period; a necessary antidote to the ethnocentricity of Western readers.

Ingram, James C.: *Economic Change in Thailand, 1850–1970,* Stanford University Press, Stanford, Calif., 1971. Economic history of Thailand following the opening of that country to processes of modernization in the middle of the nineteenth century.

Landon, Kenneth: *Southeast Asia: Crossroads of Religion,* University of Chicago Press, Chicago, 1949. Concise, reliable account which traces the spread of imported religions in Southeast Asia and their influence on the indigenous cultures and political entities evolving in the region.

Manglapus, Raul S.: *Japan in Southeast Asia,* Carnegie Endowment for International Peace, New York, 1976. Communicates the concern felt for Southeast Asian leaders for the Japanese economic "penetration" of the region since 1960. Also a useful guide to the accumulated literature on this question.

Morgan, Theodore, and Nyle Spoelstra, eds.: *Economic Interdependence in Southeast Asia,* University of Wisconsin Press, Madison, 1969. Essays concerned with the opportunities, obstacles, and accomplishments which have attended efforts to hasten economic and political integration in Southeast Asia.

Skinner, G. William: *Chinese Society in Thailand: An Analytical History,* Cornell University Press, Ithaca, N.Y., 1957. Wide-ranging survey of a major Chinese community in Southeast Asia. Informative analysis of the economic and political institutions which contribute to the adaptability and cohesiveness of the overseas Chinese in the region.

Solidum, Estrella D.: *Towards a Southeast Asian Community,* University of the Philippines Press, Quezon City, Philippines, 1974. Tabulates the diverse proposals for joint action which have been proposed under the Association of Southeast Asian Nations and its predecessor regional organization, the Association of Southeast Asia.

United Nations Conference on Trade and Development: *The Measurement of Development Effort,* New York, 1970. Useful but somewhat dated compendium of measures of development efforts with tabulations summarizing the comparative performance of less developed countries. The data summarized terminate with those for 1965.

Ethnic Diversity: The Potential for Conflict

Cynthia H. Enloe

ONE

The Nature of Ethnic Politics in Southeast Asia

Ethnic divisions in Southeast Asia are highly complex. Occasionally, the characteristics that distinguish one ethnic group from another are primarily racial—as, for instance, in the case of the overseas Chinese or Indians—but more often the distinctions are more subtle. They may include differences in language, religion, and social organization, and they may be combined with different political affiliations, economic livelihoods and status, and ties across national borders and even overseas. Indeed, in no nation of Southeast Asia is there a simple cleavage between two clearly distinguished ethnic groups. For instance, the Philippines is not made up simply of Filipinos (both Christian and Muslim) and Chinese; among Christian Filipinos there are additional factions divided according to region and language. Similarly, linguistic, regional, and religious differences split Indonesians into several ethnic groups, just as other ethnic differences divide Malaysia's indigenous peoples (non-Indian, non-Chinese) in its Borneo states of Sabah and Sarawak.

"Ethnic groups" are collectivities of individuals who feel a sense of belonging based on cultural traits—usually some combination of religion, language, and social mores—and a notion of common ancestry. The "boundaries" that separate "we" and "they" are not necessarily territorial. They consist of perceived bonds of shared loyalties and perceived differences from outsiders. An individual may withdraw from an ethnic group through a process of assimilation to another community, *if* that group is open enough to permit outsiders to affiliate through religious convergence and/or language change and other cultural transformations. An ethnic group, therefore, over generations may disappear if enough of its members opt to assimilate with some more attractive cultural group and if the society is open enough, free enough from discrimination and prejudice, to permit such cultural and social choice. But in reality ethnic groups in Europe and North America, as well as in Southeast Asia, have proved to be far more lasting than many observers predicted. Despite the homogenizing pressures of modernization, individuals have continued to prize their sense of distinctive cultural commonality. Mass media, national political consolidation, industrialization, urbanization—none of these powerful forces for change has meant the automatic disappearance of this ethnic basis for identity. In countries as different as Canada, Britain, Spain, the Soviet Union, Kenya, and Laos there are signs not just of ethnicity's persistence but even of its revival with new relevance.[1]

The diversity of ethnic groups and the subtle differences among them have posed, and will continue to pose, serious problems for governments and policy makers. Throughout the 1980s, conflicts between these ethnic groups—taking a variety of forms but all falling under the rubric of *communal conflicts*—are certain to persist in most of the nations of Southeast Asia. Although the very diversity of its ethnic makeup will probably save the region from experiencing polarizing conflict of the sort that has torn apart nations like Cyprus and Lebanon, relations between central governments and various ethnic groups will be very delicate during the next decade or so. (See Table 1 for a breakdown of the ethnic composition of Southeast Asian states according to ethnolinguistic grouping.)

This is not to say that all communal conflicts will necessarily be violent ones. Quite the contrary: ethnic anxieties and hostilities during the next 10 to 15 years will tend to manifest themselves in a

[1] Among general works discussing ethnicity are: Pierre Van den Berghe, *Race and Ethnicity,* Basic Books, New York, 1970; Daniel P. Moynihan and Nathan Glazer, *Ethnicity: Theory and Experience,* Harvard University Press, Cambridge, Mass., 1975; and Cynthia H. Enloe, *Ethnic Conflict and Political Development,* Little, Brown, Boston, 1973.

variety of ways reflecting the complexity of ethnic differences themselves. Some "conflicts" will manifest themselves as troublesome *tensions* that impede any national efforts that require two or more ethnic groups to work cooperatively (e.g., disruptions of joint agricultural programs in Laos that require lowland Lao and ethnically separate Lao-Teung to work together). Others may take the form of *political opposition* to the programs of the central government—usually because the members of one ethnic group believe that central ministries are acting as agents of a competing ethnic community (as do the Filipino Muslims, who are reluctant to comply with the agricultural programs administered by Christian officers in the Philippine government). The most extreme conflicts will be *separatist movements* in which an ethnic group or a coalition of minorities seeks to achieve independence from the governing power.

Two current trends will fundamentally affect the course of these communal tensions during the next decade. First, political authority is becoming more and more centralized in national governments as states develop increasingly sophisticated bureaucracies and mechanisms for planning. As central governments seek to extend their jurisdiction and control, they will likely become less and less tolerant of continuing attempts by ethnic groups to buffer themselves against government policies that would ultimately lead to assimilation. At the same time, however, even those ethnic groups most resistant to centralized power increasingly will need access to and influence within the central government, which will dole out more and more services and rewards (e.g., school entrances, civil service posts, and commercial licenses).

The second trend will be growing international economic interdependence. Throughout Southeast Asia foreign aid programs, international banking, and multinational corporations will affect planning and development, and thus political life in general. Policy conceived in foreign governments and private organizations will affect a region's chances for becoming a target of development policies and investment or being deemed too "marginal" to merit assistance. These decisions will also bear on particular ethnic groups by shaping their chances for achieving economic

TABLE 1
Ethnolinguistic Composition of Southeast Asian States, 1976

State	Ethnolinguistic Groups	Percentage of Population
Burma	Burman	75
	Karen	10
	Shan	6
	Indian-Pakistani*	3
	Chinese	1
	Kachin	1
	Chin	1
Cambodia	Khmer	90
	Chinese	6
	Cham	1
	Mon-Khmer tribes	1
Indonesia	Javanese	45
	Sundanese	14
	Madurese	8
	Chinese	2
Laos	Lao	67
	Mon-Khmer tribes	19
	Tai (other than Lao)	5
	Meo	4
	Chinese	3
North Vietnam	Vietnamese	85
	Tho	3
	Muong	2
	Tai	2
	Nung	2
	Chinese	1
	Meo	1
	Yao	1

State	Ethnolinguistic Groups	Percentage of Population
South Vietnam	Vietnamese	87
	Chinese	5
	Khmer	3
	Mountain chain tribes	3
	Mon-Khmer tribes	1
Malaysia	Malay	44
	Chinese	35
	Indian	11
Philippines	Cebuano	24
	Tagalog	21
	Ilocano	12
	Hiligaynon	10
	Bicol	8
	Samar-Leyte	6
	Pampangan	3
	Pangasinan	3
Singapore	Chinese	75
	Malay	14
	Indian-Pakistani*	8
Thailand	Thai	60
	Lao	25
	Chinese	10
	Malay	3
	Meo, Khmer, and others	2

*Otherwise undifferentiated.

SOURCE: Walter Connor, "An Overview of the Ethnic Composition and Problems of Non-Arab Asia," *Journal of Asian Affairs,* vol. 1, no. 1, Spring 1976, p. 11.

mobility and external support for communal causes. The consequences will inevitably influence relations among ethnic groups and between them and the state.

Both trends are likely to play a part in exacerbating communal conflicts in the future. But they will mean, paradoxically, that while the extreme form of ethnic conflict—separatist movements—will persist, separatism itself will be ever more difficult to accomplish. The more common sorts of ethnically based conflicts will be those that involve competition for the rewards of economic and social development. And since a politically dominant ethnic group can control—through the machinery of the central government—the distribution of economic benefits, economic competition among ethnic groups will likely become political conflict as well.

Just as these trends will shape future relations among ethnic groups, so another aspect of ethnicity—its susceptibility to political manipulation—will be important in determining the extent to which government policies may help diffuse potential communal conflicts. Ethnicity in Southeast Asia (or anywhere, for that matter) is a dynamic phenomenon. Persons feel that they are part of one cultural community rather than another because of important shared experiences and conditions. These common bonds can be disrupted or reinforced through political measures. Migration policies, language policies, educational certification and civil service recruitment, security controls, licensing preferences, delegation of regional autonomy or steps to enhance centralized control, citizenship criteria, land rights distribution—all these areas of government action have been and will continue to be used in ways that determine to which ethnic groups individuals feel they belong; policies in these areas also shape perceptions of which identities or allegiances carry optimal rewards or serious risks.

For the most part, governments have been more successful in reinforcing than in disrupting the sense of distinctiveness that ethnic groups have about themselves. Often, government policies intended to dissipate ethnic allegiances backfire and bolster precisely those ethnic bonds they were supposed to weaken. For example, a government's attempt to institute a national public school system can give new saliency to the lack of a single national language; of the many languages spoken by a nation's ethnic groups, which is to be chosen as the medium of instruction and exams?

There are several reasons for this perhaps inadvertent reinforcement of ethnicity, and several consequences for policy making. First, and most important, the regime seeking to subordinate ethnic affinities to a more general national identity may be seen by its own citizens as being clearly ethnically based itself. For example, the army—commonly hailed as being a symbol of an entire nation—is very often in Southeast Asian nations ethnically imbalanced or exclusivist. In such circumstances, a government's supposedly "integrative" policies in, say, language or administration are likely to be perceived by those not members of the ruling group as not so much ethnically neutral as simply favoring the regime's own constituents over members of other communal groups.

Second, a government that is earnest in its desire for equitable integration may lack symbols and institutions that are genuinely national. Precolonial and colonial administrations so thoroughly "identified" certain sectors of the polity with specific ethnic groups that independent regimes often have difficulty finding neutral institutions and symbols that are meaningful. For example, Indonesian nationalists, in order to avoid selecting Javanese as the new nation's language, deliberately adopted as an official national language Bahasa Indonesia, which was not the native tongue of any of the existing ethnic groups. Third, it is difficult for any government not to pursue certain contradictory policies. While a government may try in some areas to build up bonds that enhance national integration or reduce ethnic discrimination, it may simultaneously be administering policies in other areas which implicitly favor certain ethnic groups over others. Rarely has any Southeast Asian regime been so long in power and so fundamentally committed to *reducing ethnic barriers* that it has organized its entire government with the aim of enhancing genuine integration.

Nonetheless, governmental policies need not heighten the perceived consequences of ethnic differences and thereby make

143

communal conflict more likely. In the future, as in the past, governments that distribute civil service jobs, military commissions, or agricultural credit according to ethnic categories may motivate individuals to think of themselves in terms of their ethnic identity. By contrast, however, if all groups gain an effective voice in crucial policy decisions or if, for example, secondary school diplomas guarantee a job to everyone, then individuals are likely to see their ethnic background as less consequential.

In the following pages this essay seeks to analyze the prospects for communal conflict or accommodation in Southeast Asia. It will first sketch the most important sources of tensions among groups in the region, paying particular attention to disparities between the ethnic makeup of particular societies and the ethnic makeup of their governments. Because contemporary tensions are so inseparable from the region's historical development, it is necessary to describe today's ethnic and political alignments before proceeding to suggest several types of ethnic conflict likely in the 1980s.

TWO

Sources of Communal Tensions in Southeast Asia

The claims to legitimacy of national governments in Southeast Asia generally rest on the assertion that achievement of national unity which can supersede ethnic cleavages is the only way to ensure a state's survival and growth. This notion of legitimacy therefore causes truly nationalist governments to see ethnic allegiances and demands as "problems" with which they must deal. Those governments see ethnicity as a potential obstacle to successful national development. The Marcos government in the Philippines, for example, must replenish the scarce resources that have been drained by the Muslims' rebellion in Mindanao. Other events also serve to substantiate this common perception of "ethnicity" as a problem for hard-pressed nationalist governments: the rebellion of Shans and Karens who desire autonomy in Burma; the instability of the southern Thai border due to the disaffection of Thailand's Muslim Malay minority.

Although these perceptions are often accurate, it does not follow that the governments confronting ethnicity are therefore nationalist in the sense of having transcended all particular ethnic identities. Many central governments in these ethnically varied societies are in fact ethnic themselves—ethnic in their chief constituency, ethnic in their political and military recruiting patterns, ethnic in their perceptions of other groups in the nation, ethnic in the symbols they employ (e.g., national flags, party insignia), ethnic in their discriminatory methods of distributing the rewards of development. This is not to say that Southeast Asia has been ridden with governments that advocate apartheid or promulgate Jim Crow laws. Rather, these governments are erected on the somewhat shaky foundation of precolonial and colonial economic and political institutions that shaped the nation-states in the region and so unevenly distributed the skills and resources that enhance peoples' chances to control or influence central governments. Consequently, the prospects for communal conflict in the 1980s can be understood only in light of that past development.

BASES OF ETHNIC DIVERSITY

What are now the independent states of Southeast Asia grew out of a series of migrations and conquests. There were two principal migratory patterns. The earliest migrants moved from north to south, leaving southern China and dispersing themselves throughout what are now Burma, Thailand, Laos, and Vietnam. Some of these peoples settled in the lowlands and others settled, or were pushed into, the less economically viable highlands. The second migratory pattern was lateral, or overseas. Those peoples settled the territories of Malaysia, Singapore, Indonesia, Papua–New Guinea, and the Philippines. The earliest overseas migrants were racially related to Malays, but have been more or less "Indianized" or "Christianized" (depending on where their settlements were located in relation to the routes of foreign traders and colonists) and have adopted differing languages and modes of governance.

Of the earlier migrants from northern areas, the lowlanders—Burmans in Burma, Lao in Laos, Vietnamese and Khmers in Vietnam—have been politically dominant, occupying the most fertile territories and central market sites. But the highlanders—Shans in Burma, Meo in Laos, and Rhade in Vietnam—even though unable to build empires or control central bureaucracies, have nonetheless been far from politically marginal. They occupy strategic territories along routes of trade and conquest and thus have been the objects of both co-optation and oppression by lowland regimes set upon securing those areas for their own political ends. Generally speaking, the migrant groups that have been most politically significant in Southeast Asia have been those which have been distinct enough from the host population so as to be labeled "foreign" even generations after the original migration.

Of the overseas migrants, the Chinese historically have been the most important source of tension. When colonial administrators sought inexpensive labor, the Chinese stepped up their movement into Southeast Asia, often settling in newly expanding urban commercial centers and filling the role of intermediary, in both the towns and countryside, between Europeans and the local population. While this economic adeptness earned them the resentment of some local populations, some of the earliest Chinese immigrants adopted local life-styles, became fluent in local languages, and even adopted local family names. This was easiest in non-Muslim countries such as Thailand where religion was not an obstacle to intermarriage. However, this tendency of many "Nanyang" Chinese to assimilate into the local culture did not protect them from hostility in the event of local anti-Chinese violence, such as occurred in Indonesia in 1965 or in Malaysia in 1969. Furthermore, it often caused serious splits within local Chinese communities and thus obstructed attempts by Chinese to consolidate in interest groups for the purpose of safeguarding their well-being. Today, most Chinese are locally born and should be thought of not as "immigrants" but as integral parts of their respective societies.

The overseas migration of Indians has received less political attention for several reasons. The Indians are less numerous than other overseas migrants in most countries in the region. Where Indians are numerous—their greatest concentrations being in Burma and Malaysia—they generally have avoided conflict. In Malaysia, where Indians make up approximately 11 percent of the population, they have been divided by their own regional, religious, and caste differences: the largest subgroup, the Tamils, have been among the most poorly paid and isolated of all Malaysia's ethnic groups, working on British-owned rubber estates that often were self-contained worlds themselves. Only in Burma did the Indian minority become the center of a political conflict, chiefly because of their roles as moneylenders. The first nationalist movement in Burma, the "Thakins" (who took their name from the deferential title that Burmese used when addressing British superiors), focused on the Indians in their effort to mobilize Burmese—in fact, mainly the Burmans[2] (not the Karens or Shans or Kachins)—against colonial exploitation. As a result, by the end of the 1940s thousands of Indians fled Burma to return to India.

Colonial administrators adopted a variety of strategies to deal with the ethnic diversity in their colonies. Often, "dealing with" ethnicity meant reinforcing or increasing it—in the sense of both encouraging new migrations and solidifying barriers between already resident ethnic groups. In Vietnam, for instance, the French administered the various hill peoples separately from the lowland Vietnamese. Even though these hill peoples are a collection of numerous ethnic groups whose common interests have rarely been strong enough to make them join forces to protect their regions from outside intrusions, the French colonial administrators used a single term for them—*montagnards*. This failure to understand the subtle differences between ethnic groups whose superficial similarities make them appear identical eventually exacted its toll. In the North the French practice of separate administration actually disrupted the gradual social and cultural integration of the ethnic Tho and the Vietnamese and significantly disrupted Tho society. Having rebelled against the French in 1940, the Tho became the bulwark of the Viet Minh after 1945, supplying them with both personnel and a territorial base. In the South, by contrast, the hill tribes saw the French as protectors against incursions by land-hungry Vietnamese. Their later hostility to Diem's postcolonial attempts to impose on them both Saigon's rule and Vietnamese land laws was a primary reason for their lending early support to Viet Cong cadres.

In Laos the French followed a rather different administrative practice. They used lowland Lao as district officers governing peoples such as the Hill Tai and Lao Teung, who had been treated with contempt and harshness for generations by the Lao. Yet in

[2]*Burman* denotes a particular ethnic group. *Burmese* refers to the national population, including its various ethnic subdivisions.

the 1960s the Pathet Lao, who were Lao lowlanders themselves, found in the hill peoples—especially the Lao Teung—a source of support against the constitutional monarchy that had been established after sovereignty was recognized by the French in 1953. Having been trained by the North Vietnamese, the Pathet Lao were more sensitive than other lowland groups to hill tribe needs and community desires for autonomy. Thus Pathet Lao leaders were able to recruit many Lao Teung members to become soldiers and cadres. Another Laotian hill tribe of the North, the Meo, was divided into pro-Pathet Lao and pro-American (though hardly pro-Lao) factions.

In Cambodia the French brought Vietnamese across the borders and situated them as functionaries between the Khmers and the French, a practice that caused profound resentment.

The diversity of the French colonial approaches to ethnic groups was mirrored in the behavior of other imperialist powers during the nineteenth and twentieth centuries. In Burma the British reinforced the jurisdictional and cultural differences between hill peoples such as the Shans and Kachins and the lowland Burman community. Moreover, the British were more successful than they were with the Burmans in converting to Christianity the other lowland community, the Karens, whom they made into the mainstay of the locally recruited colonial army.

In Malaysia the British administrators felt both frustration and paternalism toward the Malays, whom they considered the "legitimate" indigenous population but whom they believed too "carefree" to supply the labor force in the rubber estates and tin mines that were the backbone of the colonial economy. Instead, British colonizers relied on Chinese and Indians for labor and recruited Malays into the civil service, the police, and later, in the 1930s, the army.

The Dutch followed the British in mastering the administrative art of indirect rule. They governed through local elites in Indonesia and maintained the separateness of the various island ethnic groups. Yet, all ethnic groups were not equally separate: the Dutch concentrated on commercial and plantation agriculture more intensely in some regions than in others, especially Java. This intense contact with Dutch colonialism made the Javanese the backbone of the Indonesian nationalist movement. Furthermore, however, the Dutch recruited volunteer soldiers from some ethnic communities at a higher rate than from others—in return promising those communities special protection from Javanese domination when the time for independence approached. Of course, as the South Moluccans who hijacked the train in the Netherlands recently reminded the Hague and the world, those promises were not kept.

Just as the Dutch developed agriculture intensively in Java, so in the Philippines the Americans went furthest in developing plantation agriculture, principally sugar, on the island of Luzon. The need of people on the island to work on huge tracts of land owned predominantly by foreigners made them more prone than other Filipinos, who increasingly were moving from rural to urban areas and thus were not so dependent on foreign-owned plantations for their income, to be sympathetic to Marxist radicalism in the 1950s. The one group that neither the American colonists nor their Spanish predecessors were successful in bringing under their centralized control were the Muslims residing in the southern islands, especially Mindanao. They were left relatively autonomous—but also economically underdeveloped—until the independent government in Manila began to "sponsor" large-scale migrations from Luzon to the south, partly to relieve land pressures that were causing more and more opposition to the policies of the new national regime.

Manila's problems with land pressures in Luzon—pressures that arose from the economic policies of a colonial regime and the disparate development of the ethnic groups that came to constitute the new nation-states in the region—illustrate the ways in which current national governments must cope with the residual conflicts resulting from early migration patterns and colonial experiences. In fact, the policies of the colonial administrators not only sustained much of the pluralism that existed because of earlier migrations and conquests, but managed to heighten awareness of that pluralism. Therefore, the newly independent regimes confronted ethnic fragmentations that were even deeper and more politically salient than they were before Western intrusion.

In Southeast Asia's ethnically divided societies some groups are currently the primary source of cheap plantation labor, others fill commercial roles, while still others cluster around certain rungs on the government's administrative ladder. In fact, the divisions are more complicated and subtle than this rough description implies. Some ethnic groups supply teachers for some schools but not others, some groups run the railroads but not the airplanes, some groups are prominent in the army's ranks but not in the officer corps, other groups have large numbers in the police but few in the army.

It is within these bounds of social and economic diversity that governments of the region—themselves often based on a particular ethnic heritage—must work to make policy that promotes security, unity, and growth. As noted above, however, the attempt to secure national unity that transcends ethnic allegiances almost by definition will be seen to benefit certain groups at the expense of, or more than, others. Thus, the conflicts of the next decade are likely to arise between central governments trying to entrench their control and minority groups whose ethnic identity is threatened by (and whose demands threaten to weaken) that control. In the following pages, capsule profiles of the states of the region sketch the current ethnic compositions of the societies and the ethnic bases for their governments.

CONTEMPORARY ETHNIC-POLITICAL ALIGNMENTS

Burma Burmans make up 75 percent of the population. Among the largest non-Burman groups are the Shans (roughly 1 million), the Karens and Kayahs (2.5 million), and the Kachins (400,000). Members of these non-Burman groups and other hill peoples as well as two different communist factions composed largely of ethnic Burmans have been involved in various rebellions since 1948. These groups occupy strategic positions along Burma's borders with India, China, and Thailand.

The Rangoon regime, reflecting the numerical and social domination of the Burmans, since independence has been overwhelmingly controlled by this ethnic majority. After independence, Karens could be found in many of the top-ranking military positions—a result of British recruitment patterns. However, distrusting the Karens and anxious to maximize their political power, the Burman ruling elite has since purged most of the Karens from the high ranks of the military. Any long-term internal peace will require reconciliation between Burmans and non-Burmans. In earlier periods, the Indian minority was a target for political attack, but today it has grown smaller and its economic influence has diminished. Moreover, the members of Burma's smaller Chinese community have been urged by Peking to think of themselves as Burmese citizens, a policy which has mitigated Burman suspicions of the local Chinese.

Thailand The politics of Thailand—civilian and military— are controlled by the ethnic Thai, who compose 67 percent of the country's population. Of the minorities, the Chinese are commercially preeminent, often providing Thai politicians with lucrative business opportunities in exchange for government tolerance. Minorities in the north and northeast are hill peoples traditionally ignored by the lowland majority. Thai Meo peoples, for example, have been denied the right to acquire titles to the land they farm, and Bangkok has encouraged lowland Thai migrants to move into traditional Meo areas. The Meo are split into several factions but currently have become the focus of anxiety on the part of the central government because of their alleged alliance with Communist dissidents along the strategic border areas. In the south the most visible ethnic minority has been the Malay Muslims, residing along the Malaysian border. Officers and police governing the provinces where the Malays are prevalent are Thai.

Laos The Laotian government since the 1950s has been controlled by lowland Lao. The hill peoples—e.g., Meo, Yao, Lao Teung—have been either denied citizenship rights or treated as second-class citizens, despite the fact that they make up almost 50 percent of the Laotian population. The Pathet Lao, the new regime, is Lao-led as well, but during its insurgency it depended on the Lao Teung for support. Thus it may have more non-Lao men among its officers at lower ranks than have previous regimes. It certainly is more sensitive to the interests of the hill peoples than Lao historically have been. The one group that still feels most insecure with the central government is the Meo, who were recruited by the American CIA to serve as the anti-Pathet Lao force in the hill region during the 1960s and early 1970s.

Cambodia The Khmers, the dominant ethnic group both in the Sihanouk and Lon Nol regimes, as well as in the new Communist regime, have historically feared and despised the ethnic Vietnamese. The Vietnamese minority in their midst reminds Khmers of their earlier imperial defeats in Indochina and of the French use of Vietnamese as plantation laborers and colonial lower-ranking officers in Cambodia. But ethnic fragmentation has not been as serious a problem in Cambodia as in most other Southeast Asian states. The most crucial political divisions in Cambodia have been among the ethnic Khmers themselves.

Vietnam In both North and South Vietnam, ethnic Vietnamese have dominated not only governing institutions but all the principal parties contending for power for centuries, ever since the southward-migrating Vietnamese pushed out the Chams and Khmers. The latter remain as small minorities. The Chinese have cultivated political adaptability under a variety of Vietnamese rulers. The various hill tribes have had different degrees of hostility toward the central government. The Tho in the North have come closest to holding significant posts of influence in a Vietnamese government under the Communists. The Diem and Thieu regimes in the South gave hill peoples only token representation. The new Communist government in the South has granted hill peoples more self-government, though it does not appear to be creating autonomous regions for them as exist for hill tribes in the North. Generally, the Hanoi regime has treated ethnic minorities with deliberate caution and will probably continue to do so.

Malaysia Since independence the dominant political force in Malaysia (and now the ruling party) has been the National Front, formerly known as the Alliance party. Originally a coalition of three separate organizations—the United Malays National Organization (UMNO), which is primarily Malay; the Malaysian Chinese Association (MCA), which is primarily Chinese; and the less powerful Malaysian Indian Congress (MIC), which is primarily Indian—the ruling party now has absorbed other parties, each of which has a distinct ethnic following. When Malaysia was established in 1963, the Alliance was augmented by similar coalitions in Sarawak and Sabah. Since 1969 the Malay dominance in this coalition has grown. At the same time, both the organization and the ethnic composition of the ruling coalition has become more diverse as the Malay elite has sought to co-opt a lesser Malay party as well as to bolster its Chinese flank by including in the coalition additional non-Malay parties. The civil service, particularly at the top ranks, is heavily staffed by Malays, although Chinese and Indians can be found in technical services. The police and especially the army are largely Malay, although the air force, which has many Chinese pilots, is less so. Certain cabinet portfolios are traditionally held by non-Malays: the Minister of Housing, for example, is Chinese, and the Minister of Telecommunications is Indian, whereas the Ministries of Interior, Defense, and Foreign Affairs are always controlled by Malays. A significant indication of Malay ascendancy since 1969 has been the awarding of the Finance Ministry portfolio, which for 20 years had been in Chinese hands, to a Malay. Perhaps the most important implication of these trends for the future is that the growing Malay political dominance will give Malays increasing influence over the national economy.

Singapore Although Prime Minister Lee Kuan Yew's People's Action party (PAP) is virtually a Chinese party in a society that is 75 percent ethnic Chinese, the government has been very conscious of both the "Malay Sea" surrounding the city-state of Singapore and the vulnerability of the finance- and processing-based economy to any regional disturbances. In particular, Singapore's Chinese leadership is sensitive to the concern of the Malaysian government for its ethnic brethren in Singapore. Thus Lee Kuan Yew has adopted an official policy of four official languages and has taken other steps to mollify the minority Malays. On the other hand, recently there have been reports that the government has "excused" Malays from military service. Persistent Malay-Chinese distrust has blocked cooperation between Malaysia's and Singapore's regimes.

Indonesia Traditionally, non-Javanese groups such as the Balinese, Papuans, Batak, and the Minangkabau have felt left out of Indonesia's political and economic system. Although Indonesia's prime ministers (unlike Malaysia's) have come from a variety of ethnic groups, the army's officer corps reportedly has become increasingly dominated by Javanese since the ascendancy of the military following the 1965 coup and countercoup which toppled Sukarno. The Javanese domination of the military is significant because the army has vastly expanded its influence throughout all sectors of the administrative and economic structure. One of the ways the army expanded its economic role was by restricting Chinese-owned businesses (Chinese are about 2.9 percent of the population). Nonetheless, non-Javanese groups might not pose the greatest difficulties for the ruling regime. Some of the potentially most troublesome problems with which the military regime will have to cope involve factional splits among Javanese army officers themselves. Also, the Javanese-dominated military regime will likely be faced with land tenure and poverty problems, which have been most pressing on densely populated Java. Finally, there is an ethnic separatist movement on the Indonesian half of New Guinea (West Irian) which is likely to impose a strain on relations between Indonesia and Papua–New Guinea.

Philippines The regime of Ferdinand Marcos is not as easily ethnically labeled as other governments in the region, except perhaps negatively—i.e., it is not Muslim and not Chinese, and it is probably not controlled chiefly by non-Luzon groups. Since the traditional support of Filipino politicians has always been localist, observers have been noting to what extent Ilocanos—the Luzon linguistic group from which Marcos comes—have benefited from martial law, particularly from the expanding role of the military. Currently, among cadets at the Philippines Military Academy the most prominent ethnic group members are Tagalog and Ilocano (both from Luzon), while the most underrepresented are Cebuano and Muslim. Regarding the Chinese minority, the Marcos government has stepped up pressure on Chinese to declare Philippines citizenship. Many local Chinese already have been assimilated, and intermarriage between Chinese and Filipinos is common. Land reform, ironically, has widened the economic gaps between well-developed regions, such as Central Luzon, and poorer regions, such as the eastern Visayas. The most disaffected ethnic minority is the Muslim community in the southern islands of Mindanao and Sulu. The Muslims' armed rebellion ended in 1977, but only after the promise of regional autonomy.

Papua–New Guinea   Despite the fact that the newly independent government is a coalition of Papuans and New Guineans, there have been charges by some Papuan representatives (the leading Papuan secessionist is Ms. Josephine Abaijah, a legislator) that the New Guineans, who make up two-thirds of the total population, are so numerically dominant that Papuans must have their own separate state to be able to develop. Papuan separatists oppose what they see as the UN's and Australia's forced integration of their territory with New Guinea. Michael Somare, the first Prime Minister and leader of the Pangu party, is a New Guinean. Bougainville, a copper-rich enclave, also has demanded autonomy, though government concessions seem to have staved off a full-blown secessionist movement there.

THREE

The Shape of Future Conflict

Within the next decade, the basic ethnic makeup of these national governments will, in all probability, remain the same. Governmental centralization and increasing international interdependency will make ethnic differences more and more politically significant, but neither trend, in itself, will alter the balance of power among various ethnic groups in a given country. There is little chance, for instance, that the Indonesian central bureaucracy—regardless of whether the military stays in power—will become dominated by Outer Islanders. Similarly, it seems unlikely that the Malaysian government will become largely non-Malay in its top ranks or that the Burmese government will be transferred from Burman to, say, Karen leadership. Nonetheless, what *could* occur in the 1980s—and what probably should occur for the sake of genuine political stability—are increases in the awareness of current ruling ethnic groups of the necessity to give other communities within their borders both more effective modes of political influence and a greater proportion of the benefits of development. It is conceivable that the governments, while remaining predominantly led by Lao, or Burman, or Javanese people, will become more genuinely pluralistic. But with the possible exceptions of Vietnam and Laos, this movement toward significantly more pluralistic governments does *not* seem likely in the 1980s.

Rather, the disparities between the ethnic composition of most governments and the ethnic diversity of their citizens are likely to continue to cause strains leading to conflict. And although the ethnic conflicts of the 1980s are likely to arise from political and economic grievances similar to those that spawned past conflicts, the changing nature of the region and the world will make future conflicts inherently different from those of the past few decades. In order to suggest the nature of these differences, it is useful to analyze three recent conflicts arising from tensions between ethnic groups.

1. The first conflict—civil wars in Burma—is the result predominantly of *deeply rooted antagonisms between ethnic groups*. These antagonisms seem to derive almost wholly from the fact that several different ethnic communities, each of which would like to achieve a greater degree of self-government than it now has, are encompassed by the nation-state of Burma, which itself is attempting to extend and consolidate its control over those groups.

Since 1948 several different groups in the nation have been rebelling simultaneously. Each of several communal groups is fighting for autonomy from the Burman-led regime in Rangoon. At the same time, two Marxist Burman parties—the Communist Party of Burma (Red Flags) and the Burmese Communist Party (White Flags)—independently launched separate rebellions in 1948. Yet the crux of the tensions that have undermined Burmese development and made Burma especially wary of international meddling is ethnic: the Red Flag (pro-Soviet) and the White Flag (pro-Chinese) Communist rebels, as well as the more recent dissident People's Democratic Party led by former Premier U Nu, would not pose such a threat to the central government if the Shans, Kachins, Karens, and other non-Burman groups were not in rebellion. The special significance of these rebellions by political parties is the constant, though as yet unrealized, possibility that they might succeed in cementing a solid alliance with two or more of the rebellious communities. To date, only U Nu's People's Democratic Party has come close to achieving such an alliance.

The Burmese rebellions have their roots in a compromise constitution hammered out in 1945 by the nationalist Anti-Fascist People's Freedom League (AFPFL) between itself and Shans and other indigenous minority groups. The Burmans, who compose three-fourths of the national population, for centuries have either ignored or scorned other ethnic groups which traditionally occupy territories away from the fertile lowland regions. But by making the cornerstone of the Burmese constitution a pledge of eventual grants of autonomy to be realized through the unified Burmese state, the Burmans were able to unite Burma's various groups and regions under the AFPFL to form the Union of Burma, which was granted full independence in 1948.

By the early 1950s, however, the minorities began to feel that the Burman-led central government was reneging on its pledges and moving toward an increasingly centralized state system. The Rangoon regime vacillated over granting the promised autonomy: a political crisis in 1958 forced U Nu to resign in favor of a caretaker government headed by Ne Win, Commander in Chief of the armed forces. But in February and March 1960, Ne Win scheduled elections in which the U Nu faction of the AFPFL returned to power. On March 2, 1962, however, believing that U Nu's efforts to fulfill the pledge were impeding national unity and economic development, Ne Win mounted a coup d'état. Ever since, he has run the country on a platform of political and administrative centralization. The Ne Win regime wants to exploit the newly appreciated mineral resources in territories inhabited predominantly by minority groups—e.g., silver in the Shan states—and to be able to have full control over the strategic regions bordering China, Thailand, and India.

The national military, which is predominantly composed of Burmans, has fought with limited success against the several ethnic armies. The largest of these is the Karen army, estimated at approximately 10,000 men, which has provided the backbone of the long rebellion. Though the rebel groups share a common resentment of Burman ethnic hegemony and political centralization as the design for the Burmese nation-state, they have been more concerned with their own communal interests and have achieved only temporary and shaky alliances among their armed forces.

This unresolved conflict has also been affected by several foreign governments, among the most important of which is Thailand, which has been accused by Ne Win of providing a sanctuary for U Nu. There have been distrust and wars between Thailand and Burma for centuries. The Thais governing in Bangkok, like their Burman counterparts in Rangoon, are very sensitive to the security threats posed by ethnic minorities residing near their mutual borders. Now that the military is again in power in Bangkok, the sensitivity of the Thais to such threats is likely to be intensified. Also involved in the Burmese rebellion are China and the United States, each of which has sought on occasion to use one of the ethnic rebel groups to advance its own interests. The United States reportedly has been supplying U Nu's party with money. U Nu has used these funds as a lure in his attempt to firm his alliance with the minorities, especially with the Karens, since he lacks a Burman popular constituency inside Burma. The Kachins and their army have been much less eager to ally themselves with U Nu despite his outside source of funds. The possibility that they might yet do so makes a united Karen nationalist movement allied with the Kachins and U Nu's supporters the most potent threat to the Rangoon regime in the 1980s.

2. Whereas in the Burmese rebellions foreign powers played largely a peripheral role—exacerbating Rangoon's suspicions that ethnic groups were being manipulated in ways that threatened the security of the governing regime—the conflicts between Meo and Lao peoples in Laos during the wars in Southeast Asia in the 1960s were complicated by *direct foreign interference* so marked that the ethnic groups became practically creatures of the foreign powers.

In these conflicts the communal interests were no less compelling than in the Burmese rebellions, but they were subsumed under external forces that tended to manipulate them to their own ends. The Meos are a hill people living in both Laos and Thailand. During the latest Indochina war one segment led by the Faydang supported the Pathet Lao, while the larger faction, assisted by the U.S. Central Intelligence Agency and led by Vang Pao, backed the anti-Pathet Lao forces. Neither Meo faction directly supported the lowland Lao of the Royal government. When the Americans withdrew from Indochina, the anticipated integration of Vang Pao's soldiers—who by then had been badly beaten and driven from their traditional hill regions—with the Royal Laotian Army fell far short of completion. Vang Pao himself was offered a post of commander in the regular government army, but there were reports of desertions among his Meo rank and file, for they probably never had enlisted with the idea of fighting for lowland Lao.

By 1970, the Laotian war had fractured an already vulnerable ethnic minority. The antagonism between lowland and hill peoples had been intensified by the creation of a CIA-trained and-equipped Meo army. Moreover, the Meos had suffered great losses in personnel and had been driven from the very territory they were defending to refugee camps in the lowlands. Americans may have gained a useful small army in the hills, but the Meos did not gain much in return. When the United States–supported regime fell, Vang Pao escaped into Thailand, leaving behind a demoralized ethnic community.

For the future there are two aspects to the Meo situation which will affect not only internal Laotian political stability but also the relations between Thailand and Laos. Moreover, both aspects will be shaped in no small measure by whether the United States decides to continue to use the Meo—and other small ethnic minorities—as clandestine, subversive forces in the region.

In Laos itself there have been signs since the organization of the new Pathet Lao government late in 1975 that the new regime, as a consequence of its dependence on Lao Teung for support during its insurgency, has brought more minority representatives into the government than has any lowland Lao regime in the past. Lao Teung are prominent among cadres carrying out political reform in the countryside. Minority leaders were also among the Deputy Ministers named by Pathet Lao officials who were anxious about the possible threat of continued Meo resistance to their regime. By December 1975, the sporadic Meo ambushes seemed to have been brought under control, but chiefly because the departure of Vang Pao dissipated Meo opposition. In the long run, the Pathet Lao will need more than just top-level appointments to cement their relations with the various hill peoples.

After the assumption of power in Laos by the Pathet Lao, thousands of Meo who feared reprisals for their activities on behalf of the United States fled the country. Some 32,000 Meos took refuge in Thailand, which has its own resident Meo minority. The Thai Meos have been alienated from the Bangkok government for generations, just as have the non-Thai ethnic groups in the north, northeast, and south. Currently, antigovernment insurgencies are being conducted in all three regions. Bangkok has followed the practice of labeling all of these insurgencies "Communist," though in fact some of them are explicitly based on ethnic grievances and are not coordinated with each other. How the Thai government resolves these conflicts will influence the future of the Meo refugees. The new Laotian government fears one possible scenario in particular: that Thailand, seeking to rid itself of the possible threat posed by Meos and to undermine the Communist government in Vientiane, might (with the help of the United States) enlist the Meos to return to Laos as insurgents.

3. The third recent kind of conflict—perhaps best exemplified by Chinese-Malay hostilities in Malaysia—is one in which *class cleavages exacerbate already existing tensions between ethnic groups*. Today's hostilities must be understood against the background of an earlier era. Early in the 1950s, Chin Peng's Malayan Communist Party (MCP) led an unsuccessful rebellion in Malaya. The British and Malayan governments were able to overcome the MCP's insurgency largely because of the ethnic distinctiveness of the guerrillas. Being predominantly Chinese in a populace that was more than 50 percent non-Chinese, Chin Peng's men could be easily distinguished from government loyalists and thus deprived of a support base. (The ease with which the government could identify its opponents makes the Malayan insurgency unlike that in South Vietnam, to which it is often misleadingly compared.) Additionally, the guerrillas' ethnic identity tended to deprive them of popular legitimacy, even if they did claim to be opposing British colonialism. A large section of the Chinese community sided with the government and supported the Chinese party in the ruling coalition.

Recently, considerable evidence has emerged of new mobilization by insurgents. The Malay-led National Front regime of Hussein Onn has tended to portray this threat as essentially a revitalization of the Emergency of the 1950s—the insurgents are Chinese

162

and their claims derive from fundamentally ethnic grievances—even though the government does make some effort to differentiate between loyal and insurgent Chinese.

Yet the reality of Malaysian communal politics is complicated by the class cleavages *within* each of the three ethnic communities. Divisions that existed 15 years ago between upper- and lower-class Malays, upper- and lower-class Chinese, and upper- and lower-class Indians have now become much more politically significant. In the mid-1950s the Alliance Party formula for tripartite governance was founded on the assumption that the elites within each of Malaya's three major ethnic groups could control the rank and file of their respective communities. But the 1969 elections revealed that both the Malay leadership in the dominant United Malays National Organization (UMNO) and the Chinese leadership in the Malaysian Chinese Association (MCA) were losing support from their co-communalists, who were poor and felt increasingly remote from the federal leadership, though admittedly no closer to one another.

The Alliance Party (now incorporating several additional parties and renamed the National Front) responded to the 1969 electoral losses and to the Chinese-Malay riots that followed by designing a Second Malaysia Five-Year Plan which explicitly pledged to redistribute wealth and opportunity in ways that were intended to give nonelite Malays whose disaffection was considered more dangerous for Alliance stability greater access to the rewards of development. Malaysian regimes have traditionally been preoccupied by the potential for Chinese subversion. Although this preoccupation is unlikely to shift in the 1980s, the new anxiety felt by the Malay political elite is likely to make politicians and bureaucrats in Kuala Lumpur far more sensitive than in previous decades to potential Malay disaffection. The politics of security have changed fundamentally in Malaysia as a result of internal divisions within each ethnic group. In the next decade or so, class tensions in Malaysia will impose severe strains on each ethnic party within the ruling coalition.

Since late 1974 there have been several Malay demonstrations against the Malay-led government. The most serious incident occurred when Malay university students came to the assistance of Malay farmers who protested the government's rice marketing conditions. At the root of the growing intra-Malay controversy is a feeling by some Malays that the success of the Second Malaysia Plan in accelerating national economic growth and expanding the long-denied access of Malays to key places in the economic structure has been accompanied only by very few benefits "trickling down" to most ordinary Malays. Crudely put, the post-1969 economic-political formula seemed to create a few new Malay millionaires at the cost of widening the economic gaps among Malays. Studies show that unemployment is about equal for Chinese and Malays; but as GNP has risen, income disparities between rich and poor Malays have grown more than have those between rich and poor Chinese.

This is not to say that the Malaysian Chinese are entirely complacent. Although the established political leaders of the Chinese seem to have accepted the political necessity of giving Malays preeminence within the governing coalition, and although some Chinese businessmen have benefited from the country's rising GNP, a significant number of Chinese see themselves as left in an intolerable squeeze by the growth of foreign (Japanese, United States, European) investment and the preference for Malays in hiring and school entrance. For instance, it has been the well-entrenched stereotype that "Malays control the government, but the Chinese control the economy." Today, however, of all the various sectors of the economy, there is only *one*—construction—in which Chinese control ownership shares. In all other sectors of manufacture, commercial agriculture, and mining it is *foreign* firms which hold the controlling shares (though often in arrangement with the government). The New Economic Plan of the early 1970s called for Malays to have 30 percent of ownership by 1990, with Indians and Chinese having 40 percent and foreign ownership to be only 30 percent. The 1976–1980 Third Malaysia Plan appears to reduce somewhat the government's commitment to such a dramatic and specific reordering of the distribution of economic rewards and influence among the various ethnic groups.

Prospects for a stable and continually developing Malaysia depend both on Malay-Chinese accommodation and on a reduction of class divisions within each ethnic group. In each case the impact of foreign companies will be significant, for those companies provide a potential means for the government to redistribute wealth and opportunities without penalizing local Chinese merchants. To accomplish their overall goals, the Malay political leadership within the National Front will seek to gain more jobs for Malays by pressing multinational firms to hire more Malays. In terms of actual ownership, however, the drive during the early 1970s to increase Malay ownership in the economy produced relatively little growth in the proportion of private ownership. Rather, increases in Malay ownership were in the form of public ownership, occurring through the expansion of the Malay-dominated government's holdings. Currently, Malay political leaders are weighing the possibility of modifying their campaign to raise the economic standard of the Malay community in order to damp Chinese dissidence and to sustain foreign investment. But such a modification might seem a betrayal in the eyes of nonelite Malays and only serve further to alienate those Malays already critical of the national government.

* * * * * *

As the previously cited trends toward increased centralization and international economic interdependence bring ethnic groups into competition for the jobs and rewards of social and economic development, the significance of class cleavages for communal conflicts is likely to become ever more pressing. Class dimensions similar to those complicating the Malay-Chinese conflict in Malaysia are likely to have far-reaching consequences for many conflicts in Southeast Asia during the 1980s. They will especially change the nature of the international dimensions of communal conflict. By this I suggest that communal antagonisms will increasingly affect and be affected by economic development.

The sort of direct foreign interference that marked the conflict between Meos in Laos and Thailand is likely to decline. Instead, the fates of rival communities in places like Malaysia increasingly will be shaped by indirect foreign influences—e.g., investments, loans, trade in goods and services, or aid—having both intended and unintended consequences. Thus, foreign governments will continue to run the risk of bolstering specific ethnic groups when they think they are only bolstering national governments. Of course, the old forms of direct influence will remain—foreign powers such as China and the United States will continue to be faced with the temptation of influencing Southeast Asian internal politics through clandestine support for particular dissident ethnic communities. But these methods are likely to be overshadowed by the modes of influence grounded in the development needs of the states of the region. Thus, in the next decade or so not only foreign governments but also other public and private actors (e.g., multilateral institutions and private enterprises) will affect communal conflicts in Southeast Asia. Why this is likely will be explored in the following section, which will assess the regional dimensions of communal conflicts in Southeast Asia before moving on to discuss broader extraregional dimensions of those conflicts.

FOUR

International Dimensions

The preceding chapters suggest that the strains arising from ethnic diversity are unlikely to be mitigated during the next 10 to 15 years. Indeed, the trends of increasing governmental centralization and international economic interdependence make the historical basis of conflicts between ethnic groups—i.e., economic and political grievances—likely to be more salient in the 1980s than ever before. These grievances, while essentially similar to those of the past, will become ever more difficult to "isolate" and respond to. They will also tend to make the international dimensions of communal conflict—meaning the effects of ethnic conflict on external actors and the influence of the involvement of external actors on those conflicts—more and more complex. For the purpose of analysis, these international dimensions may be said to take two predominant forms—regional and extra-regional—even though in practice these separate forms are often indistinguishable.

REGIONAL DIMENSIONS

In the 1980s central governments attempting to extend their effective authority to all regions within their jurisdictions will be especially concerned about activities or conditions that previously were tolerated or ignored: e.g., smuggling, the opium trade, vaguely defined borders, uncontrolled movements of peoples back and forth across national boundaries. Each of these conditions as they exist in Southeast Asia is in some way inseparable from the relations between those governments and ethnic groups. In the Philippines the government has become less tolerant of the long-practiced smuggling trade, which is carried on chiefly by Muslim Filipinos between the southern island and the Malaysian Borneo territory of Sabah.

Such conflicts involving several central governments and ethnic groups are even more clearly drawn with regard to the opium trade. On the mainland the famous "Golden Triangle" of opium trade is an international trading zone which until recently no central government in Burma, Thailand, or Laos has been willing or able to control. The principal participants in the trade are distinctively ethnic: Shan hill peoples in northern Burma, Meo hill peoples in Thailand and Laos, Chinese who are remnants of the Kuomintang army and have operated as bandits for 25 years in northern Burma. They are supported by a trading network as complex and extensive as any sophisticated multinational corporation.[3]

One of the reasons for the persistence of the opium trade is that the Shans and Meos, who have been largely excluded from participation in legitimate economic activities in their respective territories, are heavily dependent on opium as their cash crop. Furthermore, the income from opium sales has been the Shans' main means of supporting their three-decade-old rebellion against Rangoon. Therefore, if the Golden Triangle is to be dismembered and drug problems in Southeast Asian cities, Western Europe, and the United States are to be reduced in the 1980s, some efforts will probably first have to be made to improve the rights and opportunities of the Shans and Meos. These efforts could present opportunities for regional cooperation, but if a regional approach is to succeed, Thai, Burmese, and Laotian regimes will have to begin perceiving each other as partners rather than as supporters of their own dissident minorities. Thailand has treated its Meo peoples as second-class citizens or aliens, sending non-Meo ad-

[3]The U.S. Justice Department, the Dutch and Hong Kong police, and the UN have intervened and affected ethnic conditions but have been unable to crack the network.

ministrators to govern them, using U.S.-trained police units to move them out of their villages, and giving non-Meos timber rights to Meo lands. By contrast, the new Pathet Lao government has moved to bring Meo representatives into the Laotian government and has officially granted the Meos permission to cultivate opium, but under government supervision. This arrangement is intended to enable the government to contract with Western and Communist pharmaceutical firms for Laotian opium exports.

The regional dimension of ethnic disputes is most graphic when those disputes involve either conflicts between governments and ethnic groups inhabiting border regions or charges by one government that a neighboring government is giving support to ethnic insurgency. The ethnic disputes currently in progress and most likely to continue to trouble relations among governments in the region are those in the Philippines, Laos, Thailand, and Malaysia. The Meos figure in the lack of trust between Bangkok and Vientiane as much as do memories of past invasions and current differences of ideology. On the one hand, the Pathet Lao regime in Laos has grounds to believe that the Thai government will use the thousands of Meo refugees, many of whom are ex-soldiers in Vang Pao's CIA-supported Meo army, to instigate insurgencies in Laos. On the other hand, the Bangkok government is anxious to be rid of the Meo refugees and worried that the insurgent Meos within its territory will be used by the new Laotian government as a vehicle for spreading Communist influence west from Indochina. To a great extent the normalization of politics among the nations on mainland Southeast Asia will depend on finding ways to resolve ethnic problems along common borders. It is most unlikely that resolution through police operations alone will bring peace.

If normalization of postwar relations between the new regimes of Laos and Vietnam and the essentially anticommunist governments in the region hangs partly on reducing ethnic conflicts, so too does the growth of the Association of Southeast Asian Nations (ASEAN) as a regional cooperative body. Although ASEAN potentially could serve as a vehicle for solving ethnic disputes which have grown into disputes among states in the region, it probably will be unable to do so until a reduction in current conflicts enables it to develop into a truly cooperative body. The evolution will be difficult for several reasons. First, ASEAN's membership is too limited, more limited than that, for instance, of the Organization of African Unity or the Organization of American States. ASEAN does not include Burma, Laos, Cambodia, Vietnam, or Papua–New Guinea—all states whose ethnic problems could have international implications. Second, ASEAN's member nations do not especially trust each other. This traditional lack of trust has been a chief cause of continual friction concerning ethnic problems. Third, ASEAN's present members are rather chary of rushing too quickly into burdening the organization with more functions than it can handle. Thus at ASEAN's 1976 meeting on Bali the delegates were less than enthusiastic when President Suharto of Indonesia implied that ASEAN should consider dealing with regional security on a multilateral basis. The other delegates felt far more comfortable discussing the ways to increase economic ties between member states. Too hasty an assumption of security roles would most certainly prevent ASEAN from broadening its regional membership to include Vietnam, Cambodia, and Laos. Concentrating on economic cooperation should also provide all members with long-needed bases for trusting each other.

The two ethnic conflicts among its members that make ASEAN delegates most reluctant to deal with security questions on a multilateral basis are those between Malaysia and the Philippines regarding alleged Sabah support for Muslim rebels in the southern Philippines, and between Thailand and Malaysia over responsibility for putting down insurgencies by Thai Malays in Thailand and by Chinese Malaysians in Malaysia. In the 1980s both of these insurgencies may persist, the cease-fire agreement between Manila and Filipino Muslims being shaky at best. Neither rebellion is likely to topple a government in Manila, Kuala Lumpur, or Bangkok or achieve a separatist victory, but each may continue to serve as a magnet for disaffected ethnic minority members and to enable them to conduct low-level guerrilla operations. The consensus of opinion among policy makers in the region seems to be that putting these problems on the ASEAN agenda would probably sour relations between governments that are only beginning to trust one another. Moreover, ASEAN does not yet have the weight necessary to exert effective pressure on Malaysia, Thailand, or the Philippines in order to "encourage" them to settle their disputes.

Consequently, both disputes will have to be worked out bilaterally. A resolution to the Philippines-Malaysian feud over Sabah's role in the Moro National Liberation Front's rebellion will depend on Kuala Lumpur's success in restraining the state government in Sabah and in convincing Manila that it has in fact given up any claims to islands in the Sulu Sea. But the problems between Thailand and Malaysia are potentially more difficult. If the Thai Muslims in the south manage to link their small-scale rebellion with the more active ethnic insurgencies in Thailand's north, the dispute would become even more complicated, since such a linkage would necessitate bringing Laos into any resolution.

For now, at least, the questions are localized, and manageable, even though each state is preoccupied with other problems and thus unable to give as much attention to the other's border insurgency as its alleged ally would like. The focus of any reconciliation will be the renegotiation of the Thai-Malaysian border treaty. The key questions in those negotiations will be whether the Thai government will allow Malaysian Police Field Force Units to be stationed in Southern Thailand and whether Thai forces will be granted the right to "hot pursuit" of Malay dissidents across the border into Malaysia. Ultimately, though, improvement of relations between the states will most likely stem not from better police or military coordination but from unilateral policy changes undertaken by each government to persuade disaffected minority peoples that they are considered full-fledged members of Philippine, Thai, or Malaysian society, that their interests will be fairly represented in serious policy discussions, and that their particular cultural heritages will be treated with respect rather than scorned as being mere drags on national development.

EXTRAREGIONAL DIMENSIONS

Although interventions by foreign governments in the ethnic affairs of Southeast Asia have declined notably as a result of China's efforts to reach rapprochements with the existing governments in the area and the retrenchment of the United States since the end of the Vietnam War, such interventions are not extinct. In the 1980s, it is likely that direct intervention in ethnic affairs will still be seen by outside governments as a "cheap" way to exert influence on regional politics. Arms or funds can be given to local ethnic insurgencies at relatively low financial cost and with little international visibility, especially if the group aided is small, operates clandestinely, and is not monitored closely by the world press or most embassies. To insurgent groups such as the Karens in Burma and the Muslims in the Philippines, such support from states outside the region is often the difference between survival and surrender.

As these and other minority groups become more politically sophisticated in the 1980s, they will certainly seek such support. The moral question thus faced by countries such as the United States, Libya, and China is what the delivery of such support would do for the genuine interests of the ethnic groups involved locally. Many insurgent groups do in fact have justifiable reasons for making demands on their respective governments and should be aided for *those* reasons. But in the 1980s, barring rather fundamental changes in policy and orientation, foreign governments will continue to lend support not because they believe that it will actually improve the condition of a particular ethnic community, but because they see that group's insurgency as serving to destabilize a government they oppose. If so, they are also likely to continue to abandon insurgents once the groups no longer serve that "larger" foreign policy interest, whether or not local conditions improve. Such was the fate of the Meos in Laos during the Vietnam War, as it could be that of the Karens in Burma in the 1980s.

Another form of direct intervention in ethnic relations by nonregional powers that is likely to continue is military and police assistance to central governments, which is used chiefly in internal operations against ethnic dissidents. Thus the United States will continue to be a major factor in Thailand's ethnic affairs as long as it continues to serve as a prime donor of police and military assistance to the Bangkok regime, which uses that assistance in its security operations against non-Thai indigenous communities in its southern, northern, and northeastern regions. Likewise, Britain, although it has withdrawn its own forces from Southeast Asia, remains a security adviser and arms supplier to Malaysia, whose principal security operation is against local Chinese rebels.

Yet probably the greatest impact of nonregional powers on Southeast Asian communal conflicts will be indirect and economic. Foreign investors can make previously "marginal" or "remote" regions—and thus the ethnic groups that occupy them—suddenly strategically central to a national government. This in turn can generate new government attention to a neglected ethnic area, though that attention may not necessarily be salutary for the ethnic minority itself. Thus oil exploration, mining developments, new plantations, or timber operations can increase the rewards to particular ethnic groups, and the intermingling of workers from ethnic groups generally of different classes. Thus it can create frictions and new problems for the central government. Foreign investments, loans, and development aid can enlarge the "pie" in Indonesia, Papua–New Guinea, or the Philippines insofar as they create new jobs, provide new outlets for local contractors, and increase the rewards of government service. However, such foreign capital infusions do not automatically produce an equal distribution of these new economic opportunities among the country's various ethnic groups. They may widen the gap between economically dominant ethnic groups and other communities.

The states most likely to have the greatest impact on ethnic relations in Southeast Asia during the 1980s are Japan, China, the Soviet Union, and the United States. More limited roles will be played by other states outside the region such as Australia, which will be involved in Papua–New Guinea's ethnic affairs, and Arab states (especially Libya), which have lent support to Muslim rebels in the Philippines.

173

Japan Japan's influence on communal politics in Southeast Asia was greatest during World War II. During Japan's occupation of the region, Japanese officials often pursued a deliberate policy of "divide and rule" toward the ethnic groups in an occupied country. The legacy of that strategy can still be seen, especially in Malaysia and Indonesia.

Today, however, as it will be in the near future, Japan's major impact on ethnic relations is economic. Japan has become a major trading partner of Malaysia, Indonesia, the Philippines, Thailand, and Papua–New Guinea. The jobs created by Japanese companies and the lands opened by its mining and timber concessions affect ethnic relations most visibly in Sabah (Malaysia) and Papua–New Guinea. In the latter the secessionist movement in Bougainville is supported by funds attained largely through copper resources that have been developed by Japanese- and Australian-owned corporations. In Indonesia, anti-Japanese sentiments have been prompted partly by the reliance of Japanese businesses on connections with local Chinese firms. This practice developed partly because Japan began to take part in Indonesian economic development later in the postwar era than Western businesses; thus, the Japanese had to cultivate ties outside the government. Another, simpler reason for the practice may also be that the Japanese perceive the Indonesian Chinese as efficient business managers and thus the most apt joint venture partners.

China China is usually perceived as an ethnically homogeneous nation, since approximately 94 percent of its population is ethnically Han Chinese. Yet the remaining 6 percent non-Han peoples have made Peking very anxious. Chinese leaders have devoted considerable energy to defusing any possible threat that those minority communities may pose along both the southern and northern borders. This domestic concern has made the Chinese especially attentive to ethnic dissidence along the borders they share with India, Burma, Thailand, Laos, and Vietnam. Yet Peking has on occasion used those shared borders and ethnic minorities as a way to involve itself in insurgencies against neighboring governments. Currently this method is particularly notable in Burma, where China has ties with the Shans rebelling against Rangoon.

More publicized than China's own ethnic pluralism is the

pluralism it has helped create in Southeast Asia by being a source for centuries of Chinese emigrants. Regimes in the region have long been highly suspicious of Peking's moral and even material support of their respective Chinese minorities. This suspicion was not always grounded in fact, but it has made regional leaders very wary of establishing diplomatic relations with Peking.

As Peking has stepped up its efforts to normalize relations with governments in Southeast Asia, it has altered its attitude toward overseas Chinese. Chinese officials have publicly stated during visits by Thai, Filipino, and Malaysian missions to Peking that the Chinese government urges Southeast Asian Chinese to think of themselves as members of the nations in which they reside and thus to become citizens of these states. Citizenship regulations, however, frequently have made it very difficult for overseas Chinese who wanted to follow that advice to do so. In 1975 Manila relaxed the Philippines' requirements for citizenship in order to press the estimated 300,000 Chinese residing in the country who had not become citizens to do so. But in Malaysia, which has proportionately more Chinese (35 percent) than any other state in the region, many of whom have lived there for generations, the insurgency may well expand in the 1980s. This would not only heighten ethnic tensions in Malaysia but would certainly jeopardize the still-nascent Peking–Kuala Lumpur rapprochement. Finally, Peking's efforts at Southeast Asian rapprochement have been most coolly received by the military regime of Indonesia, which continues to distrust its resident Chinese and to pass laws curtailing their participation in local commerce.

Soviet Union The involvement of the Soviet Union in Southeast Asia has not been as extensive as that of Japan, the United States, and China, but it has been increasing in terms of both trade and diplomacy. Moscow has tried to exploit the anxiety of governments in the region regarding their overseas Chinese in order to try to damp the Southeast Asia–China rapprochement. But even as representatives of the Soviet Union continue to remind local leaders of Peking's potential as a subversive agent through its ties with Chinese minorities, the Soviet state-owned bank— the Moscow Navrodny Bank—reportedly has been expanding its activities in Southeast Asia from its regional headquarters in

Singapore chiefly by working through the intricate overseas Chinese business community network.

In both ideology and policy the Soviet Union's approach to its own ethnic pluralism (only approximately 52 percent of the Soviet population is ethnically Great Russian) has been one that stresses Russification and administrative centralization. The Soviets have offered this nation-building formula as a model for Southeast Asians to emulate. With two exceptions, Moscow has carried on relations with dominant ethnic groups and has supported existing central governments. First, the Soviet Union supported a Communist rebel faction in Burma. This faction, however, was led by Burmans, not minorities, and in 1975 was virtually eliminated by the Rangoon forces. Second, the Soviet Union has encouraged dissidence among China's ethnic minorities along its northern borders; while this activity is outside of Southeast Asia, it has increased Peking's sensitivity to the security problems ethnic minorities can pose for a central government.

United States Of all the powers actively involved in Southeast Asia, the United States has probably had the greatest impact on ethnic conflict in the area. First, its capital investment, which is growing steadily, has been a principal factor in the rising gross national products (GNPs) and thus the "expanding pies" which may or may not be redistributing wealth among local communities. Second, the United States has been a major donor of aid, and its military and police assistance programs have provided the governments with new abilities to deal coercively with ethnic dissidents. These military and police programs are particularly important in shaping ethnic relations in Thailand, where the Thai government is increasing its operations against groups in the north and northeast, and in the Philippines, where the government of Ferdinand Marcos seeks to end the rebellion by Muslims in Mindanao through a combination of political concessions and heavy military (the police being under the Department of Defense) deployment.

Third, as suggested earlier, the United States, particularly through the CIA, continues to be involved with some ethnic minorities in the hopes of using them as forces against governments or other minorities deemed hostile to American interests.

Currently, this sort of activity is most extensive in Burma, Thailand, and perhaps Laos.

Recently, the U.S. Agency for International Development (AID) initiated a program to determine the consequences for various ethnic groups of economic growth in Southeast Asia and elsewhere. Already the study has revealed that very few governments—Malaysia is an outstanding exception—are collecting data about communal groups in their planning operations. But this effort by AID, limited though it now is, may reflect a growing awareness on the part of some United States policy makers that foreign operations in the region have direct and indirect consequences for ethnic relations.

CONCLUSION

There are likely to be several important developments in Southeast Asia in the 1980s. With the withdrawals of Australia from Papua–New Guinea, Portugal from Timor, and the United States from Vietnam, the region for the first time in centuries will be composed of legally sovereign states. The government of each of those states will be determined to maximize its authority for the sake of implementing broad-gauged development plans. Thus the next decade will witness a significant centralization of political power and governmental activism. Southeast Asian governments will have more economic resources available to them from rising revenues and overseas loans and investments than they have had in the past. (This increase in resources, however, may be accompanied by growing indebtedness.) Similarly, governments in the region will be able to draw on more administrative and military resources than at any time since their independence—"more" not just in terms of the work force but also in terms of sophistication of infrastructure and technology.

At the same time, Southeast Asian nations will be involved in the international economic system in ways more various and complex than ever before—through banking consortia, transfers of technology, training of personnel by overseas firms and universities, and marketing systems. Although Southeast Asian nations have not taken the lead in the UNCTAD moves to reorder the distribution of power and rewards in the international economic system, they nonetheless have actively supported those initiatives. In addition, certain governments acting unilaterally have already taken steps to increase local control over foreign companies and markets. Part of the growing complexity of the involvement of Southeast Asian nations in the world's economic system has been the increase in the number of nations, institutions, and private enterprises with economic interests in the region.

These two basic trends—toward more centralized sovereign state systems and toward greater involvement with the international economic order—together will impinge significantly on the likelihood for resolving existing conflicts between ethnic groups and preventing new ones. The consolidation of the state apparatuses will mean an extension of control by central governments over the lives and territories of ethnic groups that heretofore were affected only sporadically by policies made in distant capital cities. As the groups that control the central ministries—the Javanese or Burmans or Lao—reach out to govern groups who suspect or resent their dominion, the chances for conflict between those forces will increase. If the central government's moves are in the form of police actions and land acquisitions, then conflicts are apt to be violent.

The increased involvement of foreign governments, private enterprises, and international institutions in the economies of the region is likely to have similar effects in shaping ethnic relations within the region. The opening of new bases for oil exploration on Kalimantan by Shell Oil Corporation, the introduction of mining operations on Sulawesi by International Nickel, the expansion of timber operations on Sabah by Georgia Pacific, and the opening of new electronic assembly plants in Penang, Malaysia, by Phillips Corporation—to cite but a few of the enterprises expanding their stakes in the region—will often provide central elites with new resources, abruptly transform or disrupt traditional economies in the immediate vicinity, and make jobs available to some groups more than to others. The degree to which entrepreneurial managers and embassy commercial attachés are sensitive to these and other potential ramifications of those investments will therefore be a crucial element in decreasing or increasing the chance for communal conflict. Overseas investments will have to be approved by central governments increasingly anxious to control economic planning. Thus those that do win approval are more likely to enhance the interests of the central governments than those of the ethnic communities indigenous to Sulawesi, Penang, or Kalimantan. Only in states where the central government is explicitly concerned with improving the environmental and economic conditions of each separate ethnic community under its jurisdiction will these economic developments have a strong chance of improving relations between ethnic groups.

In states where relations between ethnic groups have deteriorated to such an extent that relatively powerless ethnic groups openly resist what they perceive as a central government controlled by another ethnic group, there is every likelihood that in the 1980s conflicts will have regional and international ramifications. They may become a source of hostility between neighboring states, which seems particularly likely in Laos-Thailand relations, as well as in Malaysia-Thailand and Philippines-Thailand relations. In such instances the best chance for resolution now appears to be at the bilateral level, since ASEAN will not be ready for some time to take on the peacemaking roles that would be required.

Bilateral approaches will be more difficult, however, when powers outside the region are openly or clandestinely involved either in supporting an ethnic group controlling a central government or in aiding an insurgent ethnic group. In the coming decade, Burma, Thailand, and the Philippines will probably be most vulnerable to ethnic conflicts in which external powers interfere. But as in the case of Angola, it would be a serious error for any foreign government to presume that conflicts between regimes and dissidents in any of these nations will be merely ideological. In all of these states conflicts will be profoundly ethnic as well. If great powers support one or another feuding ethnic community, they will help escalate the levels of violence and deepen the animosities between groups that still will have to live together after the

179

great powers have turned their attention elsewhere, and, most important perhaps, they will tend to obscure or distort the real questions that divide the groups and thus make long-term resolution even more difficult to attain.

One contribution that can be made toward reducing ethnic tensions in Southeast Asia would be a reduction in foreign aid assistance to police forces—especially that of the United States police assistance programs in Thailand and the Philippines—and a concomitant increase in aid to local programs that encourage local community development. Another contribution would be made by international aid institutions such as the Asian Development Bank and the World Bank if they sponsored data collection programs that encouraged and trained local planners to gather statistics appropriate for use in determining whether the gaps in income or education between various ethnic groups are growing larger or smaller. (Currently, these data often get lost in the euphoria over gross growth data.) A third policy change that could make the 1980s a less conflict-ridden decade for Southeast Asians would be the adoption by overseas corporations setting up extractive or manufacturing operations in the region of a policy to undertake an "ethnic impact study" prior to establishing or expanding operations in a given locale. These studies should analyze which ethnic groups would be most likely to be dislocated because their land would be expropriated, their small shops would be driven out of business, or their young people would be denied jobs in favor of workers from other ethnic groups recruited from the capital city or provincial centers. Such studies by no means would ensure that companies would act so as not to exacerbate friction between communal groups; but they would help to identify the likely consequences of foreign operations for various ethnic groups before they actually occurred.

Underlying all of these recommendations is the assumption that conflicts between ethnic groups must be viewed as serious differences between groups with dissimilar cultural values and different levels of economic and political power. Based on that assumption, the definition of future ethnic disputes as disputes between allegedly rational central policy makers on the one hand and certain parochial citizens on the other would be seriously misleading. The greatest advances in reaching lasting solutions to ethnic conflicts will take place where the administrative authority to deal with ethnic discontent is shifted away from security strategists. In this important sense Prime Minister Datuk Hussein Onn of Malaysia was entirely correct when he advised his fellow ASEAN delegates in February 1976 that "our security depends on our ability to provide the goods of life to our people and to build societies which are just and fair to all."[4]

[4]*New York Times,* February 24, 1976.

Index

About the Authors

GUY J. PAUKER is a Senior Staff Member of the Social Science Department at the RAND Corporation. The author of many articles and studies on Southeast Asia, Pauker has been a consultant to various corporations and United States government agencies and has been a member of the faculties at Harvard University and the University of California, Berkeley. He received his bachelor's, law, and doctoral degrees from the University of Bucharest and has additionally received an M.A. in international and regional studies and a Ph.D. in social science from Harvard University.

FRANK H. GOLAY is a professor of Asian Studies and Economics at Cornell University. He received a B.S. in education from Central Missouri State College and an M.A. and Ph.D. in economics from the University of Chicago. He has recently served as the director of both the Cornell Southeast Asia Program and the Cornell Philippines Project. He is the editor and co-author of *Underdevelopment and Economic Nationalism in Southeast Asia* and author of numerous books and articles on the Philippines.

CYNTHIA H. ENLOE received her Ph.D. in political science from the University of California, Berkeley. She is currently associate professor of government at Clark University. Her studies of ethnic politics, Southeast Asian politics, and police-military relations have appeared in numerous journals. Among her books are *Multi-ethnic Politics: The Case of Malaysia, Ethnic Conflict and Political Development,* and *The Politics of Pollution in Comparative Perspective.*

CATHERINE GWIN is a project fellow of the 1980s Project at the Council on Foreign Relations.

191